FEAST OF FLAVOURS
from the French Kitchen

FEAST OF **FLAVOURS** *from the* French Kitchen

A STEP-BY-STEP CULINARY ADVENTURE

Elsa Van der Nest

Marshall Cavendish Cuisine

The publisher wishes to thank **Le Creuset Singapore** for the loan and use of their cookware.

Photographer: Sam Yeo
Designer: Sean Lee

Published by Marshall Cavendish Cuisine
An imprint of Marshall Cavendish International
1 New Industrial Road, Singapore 536196

Other Marshall Cavendish Offices:

Marshall Cavendish Ltd. 119 Wardour Street, London W1F 0UW, UK • Marshall Cavendish Corporation. 99 White Plains Road, Tarrytown NY 10591-9001, USA • Marshall Cavendish International (Thailand) Co Ltd. 253 Asoke, 12th Flr, Sukhumvit 21 Road, Klongtoey Nua, Wattana, Bangkok 10110, Thailand • Marshall Cavendish (Malaysia) Sdn Bhd, Times Subang, Lot 46, Subang Hi-Tech Industrial Park, Batu Tiga, 40000 Shah Alam, Selangor Darul Ehsan, Malaysia

National Library Board Singapore Cataloguing in Publication Data

Van der Nest, Elsa.
Feast of flavours from the French kitchen : a step-by-step culinary adventure / Elsa Van der Nest. –
Singapore : Marshall Cavendish Cuisine, c2006.
p. cm. – (Feast of flavours)
Includes index.
ISBN-13 : 978-981-261-171-0
ISBN-10 : 981-261-171-1

1. Cookery, French. I. Title. II. Series: Feast of flavours

TX719
641.5944 – dc21 SLS2005053662

Printed in Singapore by Times Graphics Pte Ltd

CONTENTS

COOKING TECHNIQUES

The respect that French cuisine commands today developed over centuries, and from a combination of rich agricultural resources, great chefs and a knowledgeable and appreciative dining culture. Understanding the relationships unifying these three factors is important to successful French cooking.

Blessed with astounding agricultural resources, the very foundation of a great cuisine, France produces superb dairy products such as butter, cream and cheese; poultry; lamb; fruit; vegetables and seafood; as well as fine wines.

Complementing the availability of choice ingredients, a long list of great chefs have played important roles in developing the country's cuisine, whether through culinary skill or literature. They include such individuals as Marie Antoine Carême, Georges Auguste Escoffier, Fernand Point, Paul Bocuse and Joël Robuchon. Historically, France provided local chefs with much inspiration. Before the revolution, palace cooks were encouraged to produce on a daily basis something more dazzling and more extravagant than yesterday's creation. Through this movement, the pursuit of elegant presentation also began and grew to become a quintessential quality of French cuisine.

With superior ingredients and talented cooks at one end of the dining spectrum, France also has a population of discerning and appreciative diners at the other end. Keenly aware of seasonal produce, the French know to cook and eat local foods only when they reach their peaks in flavour, aroma, texture and colour. Asparagus, for example, is eaten only in spring and is likely to be avoided when out of season. A trip to any of the many markets throughout France, whether in bustling cities or quiet villages, will reveal foods best to be enjoyed at that point in time.

Seasonal influences aside, geographical regions also play a part. As each region is famous for different produce or products, certain dishes, in utilising local specialties, become characteristic of a particular region in France. Many of the country's regional dishes have since become regarded as classic French food—the bouillabaisse of Marseilles, the aioli of Provence, the preserved goose and foie gras of Périgord, the choucroute of Alsace, the quiche of Lorraine and the tripe dishes of Normandy.

Grilling

Grilling is a cooking technique that involves a heat source that is positioned above the food. Readers accustomed to American references will know this method as broiling. American references to grilling mean barbecuing, which is to cook food items by placing them atop the heat source, usually hot coals.

To grill food properly, the grill or broiler has to be preheated very well, with the heat up high. When the tops of the food items being grilled have changed colour, indicating that the sides exposed to heat are cooked, the food should be turned over so that their undersides are exposed to heat as well. Sometimes, both surfaces appear cooked but the centre section may require more cooking. In those instances, reduce the heat of the grill to prevent the surfaces from burning or charring while the middle section cooks. Small pieces of meat and vegetables should require only brief, high heat.

When grilling, it is important to consider the distance between the food and the heat source. The food is likely to burn if it is too near, while it will barely cook if it is too far away. Timing is also important because grilling can be a very fast cooking technique. Grilled items are subjected not only to intense direct heat, but also a drying out process because the oven grill door must be left open.

Grilling is a healthy way of cooking as no added fat or oil is generally necessary. This is because meat tends to contain some fat, which drips off with grilling. Meat with less fat and most vegetables may need to be marinated in oil or a marinade to help them cope with the fierce heat. Turn grilled foods over with tongs and not a fork as piercing the food will cause its juices to escape.

Steaming

This cooking technique is intimately related to boiling, although the water never touches the food. Instead, food is steam-cooked on a plate that is suspended over boiling water by resting the plate on a partially submerged metal rack. It is necessary to have a large cooking container, whether a pot or a wok, with a snug-fitting lid for steaming. This is so that the steam produced by sustaining the water at a rolling boil can be trapped, thus cooking the food by completely surrounding it. Because the steam is trapped, its temperature is always slightly higher than that of boiling water, which is 100°C (212°F).

Vegetables and thin pieces of meat cook fairly quickly by steaming. In fact, this cooking method is most suitable for delicate foods because unlike cooking them in boiling liquid, steaming does not cause the food to roll around and break into pieces.

Blanching

Blanching could be said to be a "technique for other techniques". It involves boiling foods in water for a short period of time, usually minutes only, and it is not meant to cook the foods. Blanching prepares foods for the next step in their preparation.

Blanching generally allows the food, usually fruits and vegetables, to firm up and makes the food's natural flavour more pronounced. Green vegetables, in particular, benefit from blanching as their colour is enhanced and they look more appetising. Items such as tomatoes, peaches or almonds are typically blanched so that their skins will loosen, making it easier to peel them. Herbs are blanched mainly to tone down aggressively strong flavours and smells.

Vegetables are often also blanched before they are frozen to reduce the activity of enzymes in them. If left at their original rate of activity, these enzymes lead to spoilage. After blanching, the vegetables must be refreshed, which is done by plunging them into cold water or by placing them under cold running water to stop the cooking process. Blanching, in this instance, lengthens the safe storage period.

Pieces of offal are blanched for a number of reasons—it reduces the pungency of the item's smell; it facilitates the removal of the outer membrane because it causes the item to firm up a little and the membrane to coagulate; and it also reduces the activity of the enzymes, which cause spoilage. Always plunge blanched items into cold water or rinse to prevent the food from cooking in the residual heat.

Poaching

Poaching is another cooking method related to boiling, except that the liquid in this case is barely simmering and not at a rolling boil. The poaching liquid is usually either salted water, wine or a stock that could be made from meat, fish or vegetables.

Foods such as fish, poultry, fresh pasta and eggs can all be cooked in this way. To poach successfully, the heat must be kept low so that the liquid never surpasses a simmer and cooking time should be as short as possible. This means that the poached items, particularly fragile ones, will not break into pieces from sustained movement and will not dry out, thereby preserving their natural flavours. Similar to braising, some instances of poaching are examples of "cooking by exchange". Fish or poultry cooked in an aromatic broth at temperatures just under the boiling point allows both food and liquid to enrich each other during the cooking process. Poaching is generally a quicker cooking method than braising; it is used on better quality ingredients which require less cooking. Braising is usually reserved for tougher cuts of meat because the prolonged slow cooking breaks down the fibres of these cuts.

Sweating

This important method of cooking in fat rather than water has never been properly understood. Sweating is usually applied to vegetables such as shallots and onions, especially when they are chopped. This technique uses a minimal amount of fat and as a result, the heat should be as gentle as possible to prevent the vegetables from browning or turning any other colour. With low heat, the harshness of the vegetables' raw flavours will be transformed. This occurs as the starches convert into sugar and, in turn, bring out the hidden flavours. It will also change the texture of the vegetable from crisp to soft.

COOKING UTENSILS

In order to successfully prepare French food, certain kitchen items, such as a heatproof (flameproof) glass or copper bowl, whisks, soufflé dishes and terrines are essential.

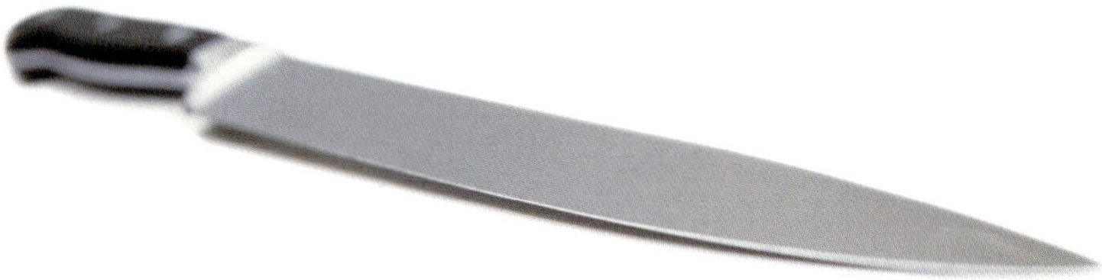

Chopping or Chef's Knife

The starting point and foundation of any kitchen, the chopping or chef's knife, or any kitchen knife for that matter, should be sharp at all times. The length of the knife's blade can range from 15–30 cm (6–12 in), but a 20 cm (8 in) blade is often the most useful and easiest to handle. Buying a set of good quality, stainless steel knives for the kitchen is a wise investment. Lower quality knives are known to warp or, worse, chip with extensive use.

Spoons

Long-handled spoons, whether made of metal or wood, are extremely useful. The best metal spoons have oval-shaped bowls that are a little pointed at the tip. Wooden spoons tend to have shallow bowls and do not conduct heat. The latter quality makes them ideal for prolonged stirring over heat.

Tart Pan

Such pans are typically made of porcelain or metal and often have fluted edges. Although the porcelain model is prettier to look at, the pastry tends not to brown as well as it otherwise would in a metal pan. This is because porcelain does not conduct heat as well as metal. It is also relatively harder to remove the cooked tart or pie from a porcelain pan.

Rolling Pin

Typically made of wood, rolling pins range in diameter from 5–7 cm (2–3 in) and may or may not have handles. A heavier pin is useful when rolling large quantities of dough. A pin that revolves on shafts, and preferably with ball bearings, is the best because it produces the most even results. Also available are several varieties of glass rolling pins that are hollow. These are filled with ice water to facilitate the handling of puff pastry which tends to collapse with heat. This rolling pin works ideally only in cooler climates. In warmer conditions, the condensation droplets are a problem.

Copper Bowl

A round-bottomed bowl made of copper, with one handle on the side, is best for whisking egg whites. This is because copper, unlike other materials such as steel, does not react with the egg whites and allows them to develop a dense texture and maximum volume without discolouring. Copper bowls come in different sizes and it is important to choose one suitable for your domestic needs. For 6–8 egg whites, for example, use a bowl about 30 cm (12 in) in diameter. A good tip for keeping the bowl steady on the work surface while you whisk is to put a folded towel underneath it.

Pastry Brush

This small brush is usually about 4 cm (2 in) wide and its bristles are typically either natural or nylon. They are useful for applying liquids such as glazes, melted butter or a basting mixture onto solid ingredients often before or after baking. Natural bristles are generally softer than nylon ones and can hold more liquid. Although nylon bristles last longer with proper care, they melt and cannot be used when they have been exposed to a heat source. Pastry brushes with harder bristles tend to leave unwanted marks, especially on unbaked pastries.

Whisks

The classic whisk is made by bending several quality metal wires in half and having the ends attached to a handle, usually made of metal as well. Balloon whisks are generally made of thinner wires than those used for regular whisks. The thinner wires incorporate more air with the beating motion. The average length of a hand-held whisk ranges from 20 cm (8 in) to 30 cm (12 in). A rotary whisk has two handles and two beaters attached to a wire frame. Rotary whisks are also used for beating eggs and are particularly effective for heavy mixtures.

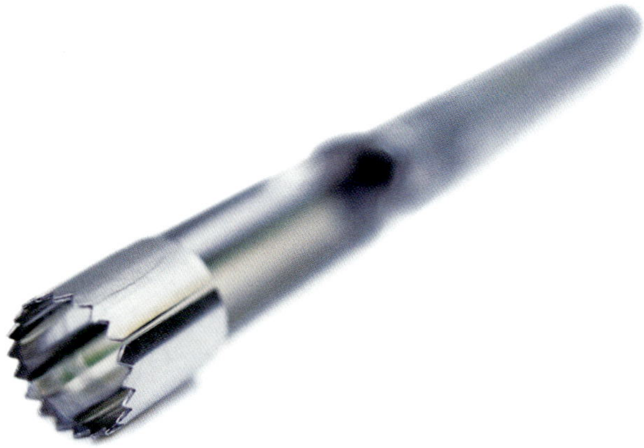

Corer

A useful utensil that allows the cook to core whole apples or pears, and hollow squash for stuffing. The corer has a cylindrical shaft with a circular, jagged cutting ring at one end and a handle at the other. Another type of corer looks more like a spoked wheel and not only cores, but also cuts the apple into wedges in one swift motion.

Vegetable Peeler

Peelers are instruments fitted with blades designed to efficiently remove peel from fruit and vegetables. The blades can be fixed or rotary but the former is generally less effective than the latter. This is because rotary blades can glide along the often irregular shape of the item being peeled and not remove more flesh than is necessary. The Y-shaped peeler (photographed) is useful for another reason. It can create elegantly thin slices of certain vegetables such as aubergines (eggplant) and courgettes (zucchini) with some pressure applied, slices that require some skill to produce with a knife.

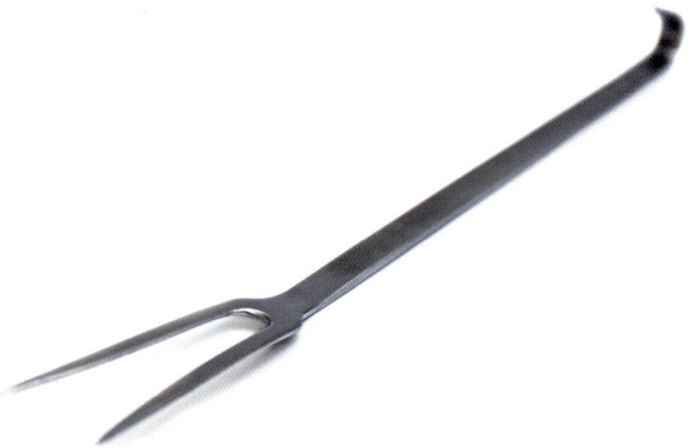

Meat Fork

This two-pronged meat fork is commonly used in the kitchen to test if foods, usually large birds or pieces of meat, are cooked. A carving fork also has two prongs but has a shorter handle.

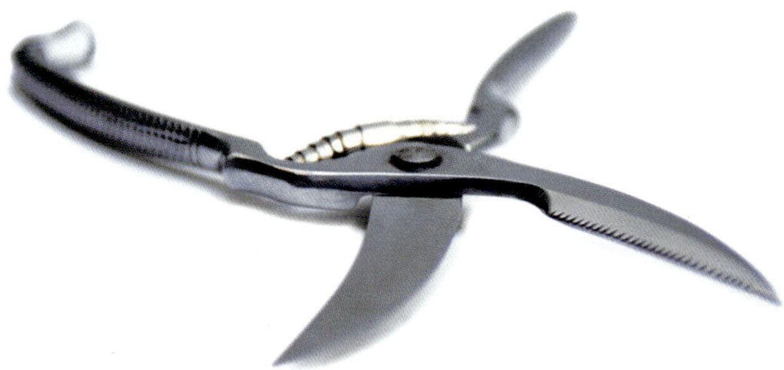

Kitchen Shears or Scissors

This utensil is especially useful in the home kitchen when it comes to cutting poultry or cleaning fish. Good multi-purpose kitchen shears should be strong enough to cut through fish fins or poultry bones and fine enough to cut fabric or thread. Some kitchen shears can be taken apart for cleaning and regular disinfecting. This is ideal if the shears are often used for non-food related tasks in the kitchen as well.

Terrine

This long and relatively narrow, rectangular mould has straight sides and a snug-fitting lid. Usually made from earthenware, porcelain or cast iron coated with enamel, terrines are typically used to cook and shape pâtés. The lids of some terrines have a small hole near a corner for steam to escape. The hole has a second function, that is, to allow a skewer to be inserted to test if cooking is completed. Apart from being long and rectangular, terrines can also be oval-shaped. While long terrines provide a neat loaf shape for slicing, their use is also more limited than their oval counterparts. Oval terrines double up as casseroles for stews and braises.

Soufflé Dish

Also known as ramekins, soufflé dishes are round with straight sides so that the soufflé mixture rises vertically as it expands. The size of the dishes varies considerably, differing in diameter and depth. As a result, the dishes are often measured by volume, which range from 120–210 ml (4–7 fl oz). The most traditional of soufflé dishes are made of white, glazed porcelain and are fluted on the outside to resemble a pleated paper case. The underside of the dish should be unglazed so that heat can penetrate quickly. Soufflé dishes may also be made of glass or earthenware.

Ice Cream Scoop

As the name implies, this utensil is specifically used to transfer ice cream from the container in which it was purchased to the serving plate or bowl. While the more traditional model resembles a flat shovel or spade, the more commonly seen version today has a half-globe bowl at the end. In the process of scooping, the bowl-fitted utensil causes the ice cream to curl into a ball. Such ice cream scoops are often also fitted with a spring-controlled blade that swivels along the bowl to help release the ball of ice cream. Some scoops have been treated with anti-freezing liquid to become non-stick, a quality that is especially useful for ice cream that is extremely hard or frozen. Scoops come in a variety of sizes ranging from 2.5–7.5 cm (1–3 in) in diameter.

WEIGHTS & MEASURES

Quantities for this book are given in Metric and American (spoon and cup) measures. Standard spoon and cup measurements used are: 1 teaspoon = 5 ml, 1 dessertspoon = 10 ml, 1 tablespoon = 15 ml, 1 cup = 250 ml. All measures are level unless otherwise stated.

LIQUID AND VOLUME MEASURES

Metric	Imperial	American
5 ml	1/6 fl oz	1 teaspoon
10 ml	1/3 fl oz	1 dessertspoon
15 ml	1/2 fl oz	1 tablespoon
60 ml	2 fl oz	1/4 cup (4 tablespoons)
85 ml	2 1/2 fl oz	1/3 cup
90 ml	3 fl oz	3/8 cup (6 tablespoons)
125 ml	4 fl oz	1/2 cup
180 ml	6 fl oz	3/4 cup
250 ml	8 fl oz	1 cup
300 ml	10 fl oz (1/2 pint)	1 1/4 cup
375 ml	12 fl oz	1 1/2 cup
435 ml	14 fl oz	1 3/4 cup
500 ml	16 fl oz	2 cups
625 ml	20 fl oz (1 pint)	2 1/2 cups
750 ml	24 fl oz (1 1/5 pint)	3 cups
1 litre	32 fl oz (1 3/5 pint)	4 cups
1.25 litres	40 fl oz (2 pints)	5 cups
1.5 litres	48 fl oz (2 2/5 pints)	6 cups
2.5 litres	80 fl oz (4 pints)	10 cups

OVEN TEMPERATURE

	°C	°F	Gas
Regulo			
Very slow	120	250	1
Slow	150	300	2
Moderately slow	160	325	3
Moderate	180	350	4
Moderately hot	190/200	370/400	5/6
Hot	210/220	410/440	6/7
Very hot	230	450	8
Super hot	250/290	475/550	9/10

ABBREVIATION

Tbsp	tablespoon
tsp	teaspoon
kg	kilogram
g	gram
l	litres
ml	millilitres

DRY MEASURES

Metric	Imperial
30 g	1 oz
45 g	1 1/2 oz
55 g	2 oz
70 g	2 1/2 oz
85 g	3 oz
100 g	3 1/2 oz
110 g	4 oz
125 g	4 1/2 oz
140 g	5 oz
280 g	10 oz
450 g	16 oz (1 lb)
500 g	1 lb, 1 1/2 oz
700 g	1 1/2 lb
800 g	1 3/4 lb
1 kg	2 lb, 3 oz
1.5 kg	3 lb, 4 1/2 oz
2 kg	4 lb, 6 oz

LENGTH

Metric	Imperial
0.5 cm	1/4 in
1 cm	1/2 in
1.5 cm	3/4 in
2.5 cm	1 in

Fish Soup (*Soupe de Poissons*)

Leek and Potato Soup (*Vichyssoise*)

Normandy Legume Soup (*Potage Normand*)

Garlic and Bread Soup (*Tourain*)

Pumpkin Soup (*Soupe de Potiron*)

Lamb and Chickpea Soup (*Soupe à l'Agneau et aux Pois Chiche*)

SOUPS

FISH SOUP
(SOUPE DE POISSONS)

Fillet fish, then slice into 5-cm (2-inch) pieces. Any firm, white-fleshed fish such as sea bass, sea bream, cod, sole or red snapper (*right*) is suitable for this recipe.

Add fish head and trimmings only after white wine has been reduced for 3 minutes or so.

Add olive oil last and in a thin stream to *rouille* sauce ingredients in the blender (processor) and blend until well combined. The sauce is now ready.

Step-By-Step

This soup is popular along the coast of the Mediterranean, particularly in Marseilles. Saffron and fennel are essential to this soup.

Ingredients

Whole fish	1, 2.5 kg (5 lb 8 oz), use firm, white-fleshed variety
Olive oil	4 Tbsp
Leek	1, white part only, finely sliced
Onion	1, peeled and finely sliced
Garlic	5 cloves, peeled and finely chopped
Carrots	2, peeled if desired and finely sliced
Salt	to taste
Freshly ground black pepper	to taste
Ripe tomatoes	500 g (1 lb 1 1/2 oz), chopped
Fennel seeds	2 tsp
Thyme	5 sprigs
Saffron threads	2 tsp
Bay leaves	3, preferably fresh, or dried
White wine	500 ml (16 fl oz / 2 cups)
Water	1.5 litres (2 2/5 pints / 6 cups)
French bread	12 slices, toasted just before serving
Emmenthaler (Swiss) cheese	125 g (4 1/2 oz), finely grated

Rouille Sauce

Garlic	4 cloves, peeled and finely chopped
Red chillies	3, seeded and finely chopped
Sea salt	1 tsp
Sliced white bread	100 g (3 1/2 oz), crusts removed and sliced
Extra virgin olive oil	250 ml (8 fl oz / 1 cup)

Method

- Fillet fish, then slice into 5-cm (2-in) pieces. Reserve head and trimmings and wash well under cold running water. Set aside.
- Heat olive oil in a heavy saucepan. Add leek, onion, garlic and carrots. Sauté over medium heat until vegetables start to soften. Season to taste.
- Add tomatoes, fennel, thyme, saffron and bay leaves. Sauté for 2 minutes more.
- Add wine and allow it to reduce for about 3 minutes.
- Add water, fish head, trimmings and seasoning. Cover and simmer over low heat for 20 minutes.
- Meanwhile, prepare sauce. Combine garlic, chillies and salt in a blender (processor) until mixture is a smooth paste.
- Crumble sliced bread, add to paste and blend to combine.
- With the blender running, add olive oil in a very thin stream until sauce is thick and smooth. Transfer to a serving bowl and set aside.
- Strain soup into a clean saucepan, pressing down with a ladle to extract as much flavour as possible from the ingredients.
- Return soup to a slow boil and add fish meat to cook.
- Drain and place cooked fish in a tureen or into individual serving bowls and ladle soup over.
- Serve immediately with the *rouille*, cheese and toast passed around separately.

Rinse leek stalks well after halving them to remove all traces of grit.

Sauté chopped leeks and onion until soft before adding potatoes and thyme.

When soup has simmered for 30 minutes, transfer to a blender (processor) to purée.

Step-By-Step

LEEK AND POTATO SOUP
(VICHYSSOISE)

A summer favourite, this cold potato soup was first created by a French chef from Vichy at New York's Ritz-Carlton Hotel in the early 1900s.

Ingredients

Leeks	1 kg (2 lb 3 oz)
Potatoes	500 g (1 lb $1^1/_2$ oz)
Butter	110 g (4 oz)
Onion	1, peeled and finely chopped
Thyme	5 sprigs
Salt	to taste
Ground white pepper	to taste
Chicken or vegetable stock	1.5 litres ($2^2/_5$ pints / 6 cups)
Double (heavy) cream	300 ml (12 fl oz / $1^1/_2$ cups)
Chives for garnishing	

Method

- Peel leeks, trimming off and discarding leafy, green parts. Make a deep slit down the centre of each stalk and rinse well. Drain and chop finely.
- Peel washed potatoes, then cut into chunks.
- Melt butter in a large saucepan. Add leeks and onion and sauté until soft.
- Add potatoes and thyme, then season to taste. Make sure potatoes are coated with butter.
- Pour in stock and bring to the boil, then simmer gently for about 30 minutes.
- Remove from heat and cool slightly before transferring to a blender (processor) to purée.
- Strain blended soup into a clean saucepan and stir in cream.
- Allow soup to cool to room temperature, then refrigerate for at least 2–3 hours.
- Just before serving, ladle into individual soup bowls and garnish as desired.
- If soup is slightly thick, thin it down with some fresh milk.

NORMANDY LEGUME SOUP
(POTAGE NORMAND)

Normandy cooks use rendered pork and beef fat for cooking, adding a distinctive flavour to the dishes from the region.

Ingredients

Dried haricot (white) beans	200 g (7 oz), soaked in cold water overnight and drained before use
Pork or duck fat	55 g (2 oz), or 3 Tbsp olive oil
Onion	1, peeled and finely chopped
Celery	1 stalk, finely chopped
Garlic	2 cloves, peeled and finely chopped
Carrots	3, peeled if desired and finely chopped
Thyme	5 sprigs + extra for garnishing (optional)
Rosemary	2 sprigs, finely chopped
Salt	to taste
Freshly ground black pepper	to taste
Puy (French green) lentils	100 g ($3^1/_2$ oz)
Green split peas	85 g (3 oz)
Chicken or vegetable stock	1.5 litres ($2^2/_5$ pints / 6 cups)

Step-By-Step

Boiled haricot beans should be soft but not mushy.

Sauté onion, celery, garlic, carrots and herbs for 5 minutes. They should be well mixed and slightly softened.

When soup has simmered for 20 minutes, add cooked haricot beans and simmer for 10 minutes and no more—any longer and the beans will disintegrate.

Method

- Boil haricot beans in water until tender, then drain and set aside.
- Heat fat in a large saucepan. Add onion, celery, garlic, carrots and herbs. Season to taste and sauté over medium heat for about 5 minutes.
- Add lentils and split peas. Sauté until they are well mixed with other ingredients.
- Pour in stock and simmer for about 20 minutes.
- Add haricot beans and simmer for another 10 minutes.
- Before serving, adjust seasoning to taste, then ladle soup into individual serving bowls.
- Serve garnished with extra thyme, if using.

GARLIC AND BREAD SOUP
(TOURAIN)

Slight variations of this hearty garlic soup are served throughout France.

Ingredients

Goose or duck fat	70 g ($2\frac{1}{2}$ oz)
Fresh young garlic	2 bulbs, cloves separated and peeled
Potatoes	2, peeled and cubed
Chicken stock	1.5 litres ($2\frac{2}{5}$ pints / 6 cups)
Thyme	2 sprigs
Sage	2 sprigs
Bay leaves	2
Salt	to taste
Ground white pepper	to taste
Egg yolks	3, preferably free range
French baguette	12 slices, toasted on both sides
Gruyère cheese	100 g ($3\frac{1}{2}$ oz), finely grated

Step-By-Step

Sauté garlic and potatoes over low heat until garlic cloves are golden before adding stock.

Beat 3 Tbsp soup into the egg yolks before adding them to the soup to prevent curdling. The yolks are meant to thicken the soup and should not cook.

Lay toasted bread slices in individual serving bowls or in a soup tureen and top with cheese. Ladle soup over only just before serving.

Method

- Melt fat in a heavy saucepan. Sauté garlic and potatoes over low heat until garlic is golden, about 3 minutes.
- Add stock, herbs and seasoning. Bring to the boil and simmer over low heat for about 30 minutes.
- Strain soup into a clean saucepan, pressing with a ladle to extract as much liquid as possible. Discard solids.
- Return strained soup to heat and gently heat through.
- Put egg yolks into a large bowl and whisk.
- Measure up 3 Tbsp of hot soup and beat into egg yolks, then stir into soup.
- Place bread slices inside a tureen or in individual serving bowls. Top with grated cheese.
- Ladle soup over and serve immediately.

Place pumpkin into a roasting dish, sprinkle 50 g (2 oz) butter cubes over and season to taste with salt and pepper before placing in the oven.

Oven-roast pumpkin at 180°C (350°F) for 25 minutes or until flesh is soft. Test by pressing lightly with the back of a fork.

Cook leeks in melted butter until soft and golden before adding stock.

Step-By-Step

PUMPKIN SOUP
(SOUPE DE POTIRON)

Pumpkins are used to make gratins in northern Italy and southern France. This rich, comforting soup is usually served during winter.

Ingredients

Pumpkin	1.5 kg (3 lb $4\frac{1}{2}$ oz), peeled and seeded
Butter	125 g ($4\frac{1}{2}$ oz)
Salt	to taste
Freshly ground black pepper	to taste
Leeks	4, white parts only, thinly sliced
Chicken stock	1.5 litres ($2\frac{2}{5}$ pints / 6 cups)
Double (heavy) cream	300 ml ($\frac{1}{2}$ pint / $1\frac{1}{4}$ cups) + extra for garnishing
Ground nutmeg	1 tsp
Chervil (optional) for garnishing	

Method

- Cut pumpkin flesh into chunks and place in a roasting dish.
- Cut butter into cubes, then measure up 50 g and distribute over pumpkin.
- Season to taste and roast pumpkin in a preheated oven at 180°C (350°F) for about 25 minutes or until the flesh is soft. Remove and set aside to cool.
- Melt remaining butter in a saucepan. Add leeks and cook until soft and golden, stirring constantly with a wooden spoon.
- Pour in stock and season to taste. Simmer for about 20 minutes.
- Add roasted pumpkin and cook for a further 10 minutes. Remove from heat.
- Add cream and nutmeg, then transfer to a blender (processor) to purée.
- Serve garnished with extra cream and chervil, if using.

LAMB AND CHICKPEA SOUP
(SOUPE À L'AGNEAU ET AUX POIS CHICHE)

This is a typical Provençal dish, with distinctive ingredients from the area—garlic, tomatoes, lamb and saffron.

Ingredients

Chickpeas	280 g (10 oz), soaked in cold water overnight and drained before use
Olive oil	3 Tbsp
Lamb chops	6, fat trimmed
Salt	to taste
Freshly ground black pepper	to taste
Onion	1, peeled and finely chopped
Garlic	3 cloves, peeled and finely chopped
Canned tomatoes	400 g ($13\frac{1}{2}$ oz), or very ripe tomatoes, chopped
Tomato paste	2 Tbsp
Lamb or beef stock	1.5 litres ($2\frac{2}{5}$ pints / 6 cups)
Thyme	6 sprigs
Dried bay leaves	3
Mint leaves	12, thinly sliced
Saffron threads	1 tsp, soaked in 4 Tbsp water
Courgettes (zucchinis)	2, cut into 1-cm ($\frac{1}{2}$-inch) cubes

Step-By-Step

Refresh boiled chickpeas by rinsing them under running water; this helps to stop the cooking process.

Brown the lamb chops before cooking them in the soup to seal in their flavourful meat juices.

Remove soup from heat when courgettes are cooked and just tender. Be careful not to overcook them as they become watery.

Method

- Boil chickpeas in water until tender. Drain and refresh under cold water to prevent overcooking from residual heat. Then drain well and set aside.
- Heat olive oil in a heavy pot. Brown and seal (sear) lamb chops on both sides, adding seasoning to taste, then remove to paper towels to drain.
- Pour out excess oil and reheat. Add onion, garlic and seasoning. Cook over medium heat until soft.
- Add canned tomatoes and tomato paste. Cook for 2 minutes, then add stock, lamb, herbs and saffron solution.
- Bring to a simmer and cook over medium heat for 45 minutes or until lamb is tender.
- Add courgettes and chickpeas. Simmer for a further 10 minutes or until courgettes are tender.
- Serve warm.

Herbed Cheese Mille-feuille (*Cervelle de Canut*)

Chicken Liver Pâté

Anchovy Spread with Breadsticks (*Anchoïade*)

Cheese Soufflés (*Soufflé au Fromage*)

Grilled Oysters on Skewers (*Huîtres en Brochettes*)

Cheese and Bacon Tart (*Quiche Lorraine*)

STARTERS

HERBED CHEESE MILLE-FEUILLE *(CERVELLE DE CANUT)*

This cheese spread is traditionally served in bistros as a light snack. If a more pungent flavour is preferred, use an aged blue cheese.

Ingredients

Ricotta cheese	125 g ($4^{1}/_{2}$ oz), drained if in liquid
Blue cheese	125 g ($4^{1}/_{2}$ oz), crumbled
Extra virgin olive oil	2 Tbsp
Champagne vinegar	1 Tbsp
Dry white wine	2 Tbsp
Shallots	3, peeled and finely chopped
Thyme	6 sprigs, finely chopped
Chives	10 stalks, finely chopped
Chervil	8 sprigs, finely chopped
Salt	to taste
Freshly ground black pepper	to taste
Frozen puff pastry	280 g (10 oz), good quality, thawed in refrigerator according to packet instructions
Egg	1, beaten, preferably free-range

Step-By-Step

Put both cheeses into a mixing bowl, then gently mash and stir with a wooden spoon to combine.

Cut thawed pastry into 8 x 5-cm (3 x 2-inch) rectangles and place onto a baking tray lined with aluminium foil.

Halve pastry rectangles horizontally and carefully remove any uncooked dough inside, then fill bottom halves with cheese mixture.

Method

- Combine both cheeses in a mixing bowl using a wooden spoon.
- Mix in olive oil, vinegar and wine.
- Fold in shallots and herbs, then season to taste with salt and pepper.
- Refrigerate until thoroughly chilled.
- Meanwhile, line a baking tray with aluminium foil, then lightly butter and flour surface.
- Cut thawed pastry into 8 x 5-cm (3 x 2-in) rectangles on a lightly floured surface.
- Place cut pastry on baking tray and lightly brush with beaten egg, then freeze for 15 minutes.
- Bake in a preheated oven at 200°C (400°F) for 15 minutes or until puffed and golden brown. Remove and cool.
- Halve pastry rectangles horizontally. Carefully remove any uncooked dough inside using a teaspoon.
- Arrange lower halves on a serving platter and top each one with a spoonful of herbed cheese mixture.
- Replace top halves and serve.

Wash chicken livers under running water to remove excess blood, then drain them well in a sieve. Trim off discoloured bile and veins before use.

Sauté livers. When livers have firmed up and browned, add brandy and simmer for 1 minute, then remove from heat and mix in cream.

Spoon pâté into ramekins, smoothen the surface and pour melted ghee over, then refrigerate.

Step-By-Step

CHICKEN LIVER PÂTÉ

A variety of pâtés or terrines is served throughout France. Pâtés are usually made from duck or goose livers or foie gras.

Ingredients

Chicken livers	450 g (1 lb)
Butter	85 g (3 oz)
Shallots	5, peeled and finely chopped
Garlic	1 clove, peeled and finely chopped
Thyme	8 sprigs
Salt	to taste
Freshly ground black pepper	to taste
Brandy	85 ml (2$^1/_2$ fl oz / $^1/_3$ cup)
Double (heavy) cream	125 ml (4 fl oz / $^1/_2$ cup)
Ghee (clarified butter)	125 g (4$^1/_2$ oz), melted

Method

- Wash livers and pat dry, then cut away discoloured bile and veins. Set aside.
- Melt butter in a saucepan over low heat, then transfer half to a frying pan (skillet). Set other half aside.
- Add shallots, garlic and thyme to frying pan and sauté until shallots are soft and transparent.
- Increase heat and add livers. Season to taste and cook until livers have firmed up and browned.
- Add brandy and simmer for 1 minute. Remove from heat and mix in cream.
- Transfer livers and pan juices to a blender (processor). Blend until smooth while adding remaining melted butter.
- Spoon pâté into a terrine dish or ramekins and smoothen the surface(s).
- Pour ghee over to seal pâté, then place in the refrigerator to set.
- Serve with toast, brioche or spooned into profiteroles.

ANCHOVY SPREAD WITH BREADSTICKS *(ANCHOÏADE)*

This pungent paste originated from France's southern coast, which is home to the country's anchovy fishing industries.

Ingredients

Salted anchovy fillets	100 g ($3^1/_2$ oz)
Black olives	55 g (2 oz), pitted and chopped
Garlic	4 cloves, peeled and chopped
Parsley	6 sprigs, finely chopped
Thyme	8 sprigs, finely chopped
Salt	to taste
Freshly ground black pepper	to taste
Red wine or balsamic vinegar	1 Tbsp
Extra virgin olive oil	180 ml (6 fl oz / $^3/_4$ cup)
Store-bought breadsticks	10

Step-By-Step

Pit olives before use, then finely chop.

Rinse anchovy fillets to remove excess salt and drain well before use. Do not over-rinse or some of the flavour will be washed away as well.

After adding vinegar to ingredients in the blender (processor), add olive oil in a thin stream until paste is very thick.

Method

- Rinse anchovies under cold running water to remove all traces of salt.
- Combine anchovies, olives, garlic, herbs and seasoning using a mortar and pestle. Alternatively, use a blender (processor) until mixture is a paste.
- Add vinegar and pound or blend for a few seconds more.
- While pounding or the machine is running, add olive oil in a thin stream until paste is very thick.
- Serve with breadsticks or sliced raw vegetables.

CHEESE SOUFFLÉS
(SOUFFLE AU FROMAGE)

Undoubtedly the most classic of all soufflés, this one is made with Gruyère but Emmenthaler and Comté also produce excellent results.

Ingredients

Soufflé dishes or ramekins	6–8
Butter	40 g (1 1/4 oz) + extra for greasing
Milk	250 ml (8 fl oz / 1 cup)
Plain (all-purpose) flour	40 g (1 1/2 oz)
Egg yolks	3
Gruyère cheese	100 g (3 1/2 oz), finely grated
Double (heavy) cream	1 Tbsp
Ground nutmeg	a pinch
Salt	to taste
Ground white pepper	to taste
Egg whites	4

Step-By-Step

After stirring hot milk into butter and flour mixture, remove from heat and whisk in egg yolks, one at a time.

Beat egg whites either by hand or in a cake mixer until soft peaks form, then whisk one-quarter into the above mixture.

Spoon soufflé mixture into buttered, chilled ramekins or soufflé dishes.

Method

- Prepare porcelain soufflé dishes or ramekins for use. Generously butter insides and refrigerate until needed.
- Pour milk into a saucepan and gently heat through over low heat; do not boil.
- Melt 40 g (1 1/4 oz) butter in another saucepan over low heat. Add flour and stir for 1 minute.
- Add hot milk in a thin stream, stirring constantly. Cook mixture, still over low heat, until it thickens.
- Remove from heat and whisk in egg yolks, one at a time.
- Mix in cheese, cream, nutmeg and seasoning to taste.
- Separately beat egg whites until soft peaks form.
- Whisk one-quarter of beaten egg whites into mixture in the saucepan, then pour combined mixture into remaining egg whites.
- Gently fold mixture into egg whites, then spoon into soufflé dishes or ramekins until three-quarters way full.
- Place soufflé dishes or ramekins in an ovenproof dish and fill with water until they are half submerged.
- Bake in a preheated oven at 200°C (400°F) for 15–20 minutes or until well risen and golden brown on top.
- Serve immediately.

Remove oysters from their shells and place in a clean sieve set over the bowl of oyster juice collected earlier so none is wasted.

Wrap each oyster with a slice of bacon and thread 2 onto a skewer. Position them near the tip for easier lifting later.

Step-By-Step

GRILLED OYSTERS ON SKEWERS
(HUÎTRES EN BROCHETTES)

Oysters are popular in France and these fresh molluscs go well with French champagne.

Ingredients

Oysters	24, large
White wine	4 Tbsp
Bacon	24 thin slices, rind and fat trimmed
Bamboo skewers	12
Olive oil	
Lemon wedges	

Cheese Topping (combined)

Dry breadcrumbs	3 Tbsp
Finely grated Gruyère cheese	3 Tbsp
Cayenne pepper	a pinch or more to taste

Method

- Carefully open each oyster shell and pass the juice through a fine sieve set on top of a bowl.
- Clean sieve and replace over bowl.
- Remove oysters from their shells and place in sieve to collect any remaining juice. Discard shells.
- Combine wine and oyster juice in a saucepan and bring to a gentle boil.
- As soon as the liquid begins to bubble, add oysters and gently poach for 6 seconds.
- Remove from heat and drain oysters using a fine sieve. Refresh them under running water.
- Wrap each oyster with a slice of bacon, then thread 2 onto a skewer.
- Grease a grill pan with olive oil and place over moderate–high heat.
- Place skewers on hot pan for grill marks, turning from time to time.
- Transfer skewers to a baking tray and sprinkle with cheese topping.
- Place baking tray under a hot oven-grill until bacon is crisp.
- Serve on a platter with lemon wedges; diners add a squeeze of lemon over before eating.

CHEESE AND BACON TART
(QUICHE LORRAINE)

Quiche Lorraine is a regional dish from Nancy, Lorraine. The origin of this tart reputedly dates as far back as the seventeenth century.

Ingredients

Shortcrust pastry	280 g (10 oz)
Eggs	3, extra large, preferably free-range
Crème fraîche	250 ml (8 fl oz / 1 cup)
Salt	to taste
Freshly ground black pepper	to taste
Ground nutmeg	1 tsp
Greaseproof paper	
Rice grains	1 kg
Butter	55 g (2 oz)
Back bacon	300 g ($10\frac{1}{2}$ oz), sliced into 2.5-cm (1-in) pieces

Step-By-Step

After rolling out pastry to desired thickness, line tart pan and trim off excess by running a rolling pin over the top.

Line chilled pastry shell with greaseproof paper and fill with rice grains before baking blind, or without its intended filling.

Fill baked pastry shell with fried bacon pieces, making sure they are evenly distributed, before pouring in egg mixture.

Method

- Roll out pastry to desired thickness and line a buttered tart pan 24 cm (10 in) in diameter. Trim off excess and refrigerate for 20 minutes.
- Combine eggs, crème fraîche, seasoning and nutmeg in a large bowl. Whisk until well blended. Set aside.
- Line chilled pastry shell with greaseproof paper and fill with rice grains.
- Bake pastry blind in a preheated oven at 200°C (400°F) for 10 minutes.
- Meanwhile, melt butter in a pan and fry bacon until golden. Drain on paper towels.
- Take pastry out of the oven and remove paper and rice grains.
- Bake empty shell for a further 5 minutes, then remove and cool completely.
- Fill pastry shell with bacon and pour egg mixture over.
- Bake for about 30 minutes or until lightly browned and firm.
- Allow quiche to cool for 10 minutes before slicing into wedges to serve.

VEGETABLES & SALADS

Lentils with Foie Gras and Quail Eggs

Salad with Bacon and Croutons (*Salade aux Noix*)

Tuna Salad (*Salade Niçoise*)

Classic Piperade

Asparagus with Hollandaise Sauce

Potato Gratin, Dauphine Style (*Gratin Dauphinois*)

Ratatouille

Leeks with Olive Oil and Lemon Juice

LENTILS WITH FOIE GRAS AND QUAIL EGGS

Foie gras, with its unique and luxuriously rich taste, is regarded as a delicacy throughout France and is used in a variety of recipes.

Ingredients

Brown lentils	100 g, soaked in cold water for 10 hours and drained before use
Bouquet garni	100 g (3 1/2 oz), consisting of thyme, parsley and celery leaves
Dried bay leaves	3
Butter	60 g (2 oz)
Truffle juice	1 Tbsp
Salt	to taste
Freshly ground black pepper	to taste
Foie gras terrine	140 g (5 oz), cut into 8–10 slices
Quail eggs	8–10
Baby rocket (arugula) leaves	50 g (2 oz)
Extra virgin olive oil	85 ml (2 1/2 fl oz / 1/3 cup)

Step-By-Step

Cut foie gras terrine into slices about 6 x 4 cm (2 1/2 x 1 1/2 inch) and set aside.

Fry quail eggs in the foie gras fat left in the pan for extra flavour.

Toss rocket leaves in olive oil only just before serving. Dressed salad leaves have to be served immediately.

Method

- Rinse pre-soaked lentils and drain well.
- Put lentils, bouquet garni and bay leaves into a saucepan. Add enough cold water to cover ingredients.
- Bring to a slow boil and simmer gently for 20–25 minutes.
- Drain cooked lentils, discarding bouquet garni and bay leaves.
- Mix in 40 g (1 1/4 oz) butter and truffle juice. Season to taste. Set aside.
- Heat remaining butter in a non-stick pan. Fry foie gras over moderate–low heat for 30 seconds on each side. Dish out.
- Use the foie gras fat left in the pan, adding a knob of butter if necessary, to fry each quail egg into a sunny-side up. Dish out, cool and trim jagged edges.
- Toss rocket leaves in olive oil just before serving.
- To serve, divide lentils and foie gras among individual serving plates and top with baby rocket and fried quail eggs.

Step-By-Step

Rub the bread slices with garlic before grilling to give them some added flavour.

For salad dressing, combine walnut oil, red wine vinegar and Dijon mustard. Add olive oil last and in a thin stream, whisking continuously.

Fry the walnuts in the residual bacon fat to give them an irresistible aroma of fried bacon.

SALAD WITH BACON AND CROUTONS
(SALADE AUX NOIX)

Walnut oil is used in many dressings. This particular salad is typically served at lunch in the summer with a chilled glass of French wine.

Ingredients

Baguette	8 thin slices
Garlic	1 clove, peeled and halved
Walnuts	70 g ($2\frac{1}{2}$ oz), roughly chopped
Streaky bacon	280 g (10 oz), sliced into strips
Mesclun leaves	150 g (5 oz)

Dressing

Walnut oil	1 Tbsp
Red wine vinegar	1 Tbsp
Dijon mustard	1 tsp
Extra virgin olive oil	85 ml ($2\frac{1}{2}$ fl oz / $\frac{1}{3}$ cup)

Method

- Preheat oven-grill and rub bread slices with garlic. Drizzle a little olive oil on each side and grill until golden brown. Remove and leave to cool.
- Prepare dressing. Combine walnut oil, vinegar and mustard in a bowl. Whisk in remaining olive oil, adding in a thin stream. Season to taste, if necessary and set aside.
- Immerse walnuts in boiling hot water and let stand for 1 minute, then drain in a colander and shake dry. Set aside.
- Sauté bacon in a dry frying pan (skillet) until crisp. Remove with a slotted spoon and drain on paper towels.
- Fry walnuts in the bacon fat left in the pan for about 2 minutes or until golden, then dish out.
- Place salad leaves in a large bowl and sprinkle bacon and walnuts over.
- Pour dressing into the same pan and heat through, then pour over salad and toss well.
- Lastly, add garlic croutons and serve. Alternatively, line a serving platter with the croutons and top with tossed salad.

Boil eggs in water for 5 minutes, then drain and refresh under cold running water, or plunge into cold water for 3 minutes.

The amount of lettuce used should be about half the volume of the whole salad. Adjust accordingly.

Transfer dressed lettuce leaves to a serving platter, then top as desired with all remaining solid ingredients. Drizzle olive oil over to finish.

Step-By-Step

TUNA SALAD
(SALADE NIÇOISE)

The phrase "*à la Niçoise*" refers to dishes typical of Nice. The region's cuisine customarily uses tomatoes, olives, garlic and anchovies.

Ingredients

New potatoes	12, peeled if desired
French beans	225 g (8 oz), strings removed and left whole
Cos (romaine) lettuce	4 small heads, or lettuce of choice
Canned anchovy fillets in oil	55 g (2 oz), drained
Black olives	20, pitted
Plum (Roma) tomatoes	4, large, ripe, sliced into wedges
Eggs	4, preferably free-range, hard-boiled, shelled and quartered
Canned tuna in olive oil	225 g (8 oz), drained and flaked into chunks, use best quality available
Extra virgin olive oil	to taste

Anchovy Dressing

Egg	1
Garlic	1 clove, peeled
Flat-leaf (Italian) parsley	a handful or more to taste
Canned anchovy fillets	55 g (2 oz), drained
Lemon juice	squeezed from 1 lemon
Tomato sauce (ketchup)	1 Tbsp
Sunflower oil	250 ml (8 fl oz / 1 cup)
Extra virgin olive oil	75 ml ($2^1/_2$ fl oz / 5 Tbsp)
Freshly ground black pepper	to taste

Method

- Boil potatoes in salted water until just tender. Drain and set aside.
- Lower French beans into rapidly boiling water to cook, then refresh under running water. Set aside.
- Discard outer leaves of lettuce and separate the rest. Wash and dry.
- Prepare anchovy dressing. Combine all ingredients, except oils and pepper, in a blender (processor) and blend mixture into a smooth paste.
- With the blender running, add sunflower oil in a thin stream through the feeder tube. Repeat with olive oil.
- Dressing should have the consistency of double (heavy) cream. Season to taste with pepper.
- Separately dress lettuce leaves, potatoes and beans to taste.
- Transfer lettuce to a serving platter, forming a 'bed'.
- Top as desired with potatoes, beans, anchovies, olives, tomatoes, eggs and tuna. Trim eggs of excess white, if desired.
- Drizzle olive oil over and serve with country bread.

Slice courgette into 2.5-cm (1-in) rolls and set aside.

To prepare capsicum for use, first cut it open and deseed, then slice into 2.5-cm (1-in) wide pieces.

After removing vegetables from the pan, add olives and basil to sauce left in the pan and stir through to mix.

Step-By-Step

CLASSIC PIPERADE

This recipe is versatile; it can be served as a warm salad for lunch or as a vegetable dish for dinner.

Ingredients

Extra virgin olive oil	125 ml (4 fl oz / $^{1}/_{2}$ cup)
Courgette (zucchini)	1, large, sliced into 2.5-cm (1-in) rolls
Aubergine (eggplant/brinjal)	1, medium, sliced into 2.5-cm (1-in) rolls
Shallots	8, small, peeled
Baby fennel bulbs	4, trimmed
Red capsicum (bell pepper)	1, seeded and cut into 2.5-cm (1-in) wide pieces
Yellow capsicum	1, seeded and cut into 2.5-cm (1-in) wide pieces
Green capsicum	1, seeded and cut into 2.5-cm (1-in) wide pieces
Garlic	1 whole pod, cloves separated and peeled
Tomato juice	100 ml (3$^{1}/_{2}$ fl oz)
Freshly ground salt	to taste
Freshly ground black pepper	to taste
Black olives	125 g (4$^{1}/_{2}$ oz)
Basil leaves	20
Medium-boiled eggs	4, halved and trimmed of excess white if desired

Method

- Heat olive oil in a pan. Add courgette, aubergine, shallots, fennel and capsicums. Sauté until tender.
- Add garlic, tomato juice and seasoning to taste.
- Cover pan with a tight-fitting lid and cook over low heat until vegetables are just soft to the touch. Switch off heat.
- Remove vegetables to a serving bowl or plate.
- Add olives and basil to pan and stir through, then add to vegetables together with any remaining sauce.
- Top as desired with eggs and serve warm.

Asparagus does not require much cooking. Cook for only 3–4 minutes in simmering salted water.

Use only a heatproof (flameproof) glass bowl for making the sauce. This is because a metal bowl will cause the egg yolks to discolour.

Add melted butter to the sauce gradually and whisk continuously to blend well.

Step-By-Step

ASPARAGUS WITH HOLLANDAISE SAUCE

The recipe for hollandaise sauce can be used with many other dishes, especially those involving fish, vegetables and eggs.

Ingredients

Asparagus	600 g (1 lb 5 oz), washed
Butter	180 g (6 oz), cubed and placed in the freezer until needed
Egg yolks	3
Water	1 Tbsp
Lemon juice	1 Tbsp
Salt	to taste
Ground white pepper	to taste

Method

- Trim lower ends of asparagus and peel tough outer layers.
- Cook asparagus in a large pan of simmering salted water for 3–4 minutes. Avoid a rapid boil as the asparagus will lose crispness and colour. Drain and refresh under running water.
- Melt 25 g (1 oz) butter in a small saucepan over low heat. Set aside.
- Place a bain-marie, or a half-filled pot of water with a heatproof (flameproof) glass bowl set on top, over low heat.
- Add egg yolks and water to glass bowl and whisk for 1–2 minutes or until foamy.
- Add half the cold butter and whisk for 1 minute.
- Whisk in remaining butter and remove bain-marie from heat; the mixture should look smooth and creamy.
- Gradually add melted butter, whisking continuously until sauce is thick.
- Beat in lemon juice and season to taste with salt and pepper.
- If sauce curdles during cooking process, remove from heat immediately, then place an extra egg yolk in a clean bowl and gradually whisk sauce into it.
- If sauce is too thick, add 1–2 tsp hot water to remedy.
- Arrange asparagus on a serving plate and spoon sauce over.
- Serve warm.

POTATO GRATIN, DAUPHINE STYLE
(GRATIN DAUPHINOIS)

There are several versions of this dish from Dauphine in southeastern France; some recipes are without the cheese topping.

Ingredients

Garlic	1 clove or more to taste, peeled and minced
Milk	125 ml (4 fl oz / 1/2 cup)
Double (heavy) cream	300 ml (1/2 pint / 1 1/4 cups)
Ground cinnamon	1/2 tsp
Ground nutmeg	1/2 tsp
Salt	to taste
Freshly ground black pepper	to taste
Potatoes for boiling	500 g (1 lb 1 1/2 oz)
Butter for greasing	
Gruyère cheese	85 g (3 oz), grated

Step-By-Step

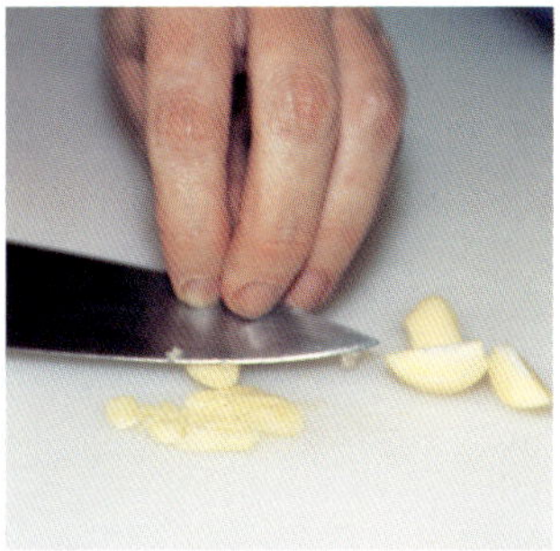

Crush garlic with the side of a knife to make the process of mincing easier.

Drain boiled potatoes and refresh under running water, then pat dry with a clean kitchen towel.

Place potato slices into buttered baking dish, arranging in neat rows, before adding cream mixture and cheese.

Method

- Combine garlic, milk, cream, cinnamon, nutmeg and seasoning in a large saucepan. Bring to the boil over low heat and remove.
- Meanwhile, peel and wash potatoes, then parboil for 5 minutes.
- Drain and refresh potatoes, then pat dry with a kitchen towel. Slice into 0.5-cm (1/4-in) thick slices.
- Butter a 26 x 18-cm (10 x 7-in) baking dish. Arrange potato slices in neat rows and pour warm cream mixture over. Sprinkle with grated cheese.
- Bake in a preheated oven at 190°C (370°F) until golden brown, about 35–40 minutes.
- Serve warm from the baking dish.

RATATOUILLE

Ratatouille is the French word for "mix" and this dish makes a great vegetable accompaniment to many meals.

Ingredients

Aubergines (eggplants/brinjals)	2, large, chopped
Salt	
Olive oil	125 ml (4 fl oz / 1/2 cup)
Red onions	3, medium, peeled and thinly sliced
Garlic	3 cloves, peeled and sliced
Dried bay leaves	2
Thyme	6 sprigs, finely chopped
Flat-leaf (Italian) parsley	10 sprigs, finely chopped
Courgettes (zucchinis)	2, diced
Red capsicum (bell pepper)	1, seeded and cut into 2.5-cm (1-in) squares
Yellow capsicum	1, seeded and cut into 2.5-cm (1-in) squares
Green capsicum	1, seeded and cut into 2.5-cm (1-in) squares
Canned tomatoes	350 g (12 oz), roughly chopped
Tomato paste	2 Tbsp
Sugar	5 g
Black olives	150 g (5 oz), pitted if desired and left whole
Extra virgin olive oil	to taste
Freshly ground black pepper	to taste

Step-By-Step

Place a plate on top of chopped aubergines after sprinkling with salt so that more liquid will be drained out with the added weight.

Sauté each vegetable separately before mixing them together with canned tomatoes, tomato paste, sugar and olives.

When the cooked dish has cooled slightly, drizzle in extra olive oil to taste and serve.

Method

- Sprinkle aubergines with salt, then weigh down with a plate and set aside for 15 minutes for excess liquid to drain out.
- Rinse drained aubergines well and pat dry with paper towels. Set aside.
- Heat olive oil in a casserole over medium heat. Add a small knob of butter for added flavour, if desired.
- Sauté onions, garlic and herbs until softened, then dish out.
- Sauté courgettes in the same casserole over medium heat for a few minutes or until softened, then dish out.
- Repeat with capsicums, then aubergines.
- Combine all sautéed ingredients, canned tomatoes, tomato paste, sugar and olives in the casserole. Mix well.
- Bake in a preheated oven at 180°C (350°F) for 40 minutes.
- When done, set aside to cool and drizzle over extra virgin olive oil to taste and season with black pepper.
- To serve, either spoon onto a platter or divide into individual portions.

LEEKS WITH OLIVE OIL AND LEMON JUICE

Leeks are available throughout the year which makes this easy-to-prepare, tasty and aromatic dish a winner all around.

Ingredients

Extra virgin olive oil	2 Tbsp
White wine	1 Tbsp
Tomato paste	1 tsp or more to taste
Rosemary leaves	from 6 sprigs or to taste
Garlic	4 cloves, peeled
Coriander seeds	5 g, coarsely crushed
Brown sugar	1 Tbsp
Water	250 ml (8 fl oz / 1 cup)
Leeks	6, trimmed
Lemon juice	1 tsp
Salt	to taste
Ground black pepper	to taste
Chopped parsley	2 Tbsp

Step-By-Step

Combine olive oil, wine, tomato paste, rosemary, garlic, coriander seeds, sugar and water in a large pan and bring to the boil.

When liquid has reached the boil, reduce heat to a simmer and add leeks. Cook for 15–20 minutes, depending on the age of the leeks, until just tender.

Just before removing leeks, add lemon juice and gently stir through, then remove leeks to a serving plate.

Method

- Combine olive oil, wine, tomato paste, rosemary, garlic, coriander, sugar and water in a large pan. Bring to the boil.
- Reduce heat and add leeks. Simmer for 15–20 minutes or until just tender.
- Just before removing leeks, add lemon juice and lightly stir through.
- Transfer cooked leeks to a serving plate of choice.
- Reduce liquid for 1 minute and season to taste with salt and pepper.
- Spoon sauce over leeks and serve garnished with parsley.

SEAFOOD

Scallops with Beurre Blanc Sauce (*Coquilles Saint-Jacques au Beurre Blanc*)

Mussels with White Wine (*Moules Marinieres*)

Stuffed Squid (*Chipirons Farcis*)

Langoustines in Curry Sauce (*Langoustines au Curry*)

Lobster Thermidor

Bourride of Snapper, Sète Style

Sea Bass with Stuffing (*Bar Farci*)

Baked Salmon in Paper with Basil Sauce (*Saumon au Pistou en Papillote*)

To prepare scallops for use, first rinse under cold running water, then pat dry with paper towels.

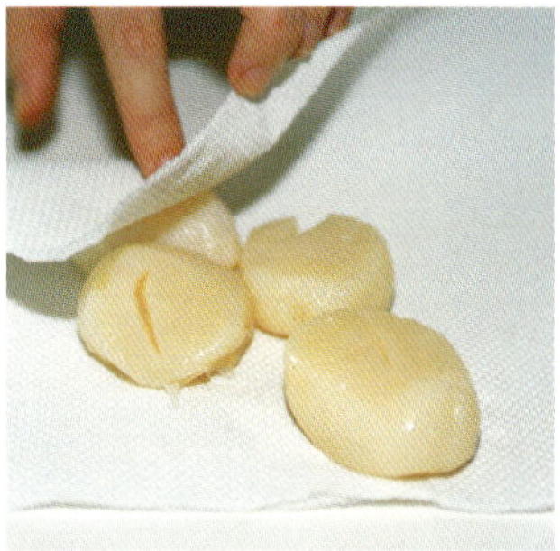

Combine shallots, wine, vinegar and seasoning in a saucepan, then simmer until liquid is reduced to about 1 Tbsp.

After incorporating butter into reduction, simmer until it is light and creamy; *beurre blanc* sauce is now ready.

Step-By-Step

SCALLOPS WITH BEURRE BLANC SAUCE
(COQUILLES SAINT-JACQUES AU BEURRE BLANC)

Beurre blanc is one of the classic French sauces. It is a reduction of French shallots and vinegar, with butter incorporated into it.

Ingredients

Sea scallops	12, large
Shallots	3, peeled and thinly sliced
Chardonnay	90 ml (3 fl oz / 6 Tbsp)
White wine vinegar	3 Tbsp
Salt	a pinch
Ground white pepper	a pinch
Cold butter	200 g (7 oz), cubed
Finely chopped parsley	2 Tbsp

Method

- Rinse scallops gently under running water, then pat dry with paper towels.
- Combine shallots, chardonnay, vinegar and seasoning in a saucepan. Bring to a simmer and reduce until about 1 Tbsp liquid remains.
- With saucepan still over low heat, gradually whisk in 180 g (6 oz) butter, piece by piece.
- When all of the butter has been incorporated and the *beurre blanc* is light and creamy, remove from heat and set aside.
- Melt remaining butter in a non-stick frying pan (skillet). Cook scallops over moderate heat for 2 minutes on each side.
- Place cooked scallops on a serving platter. Spoon sauce over and garnish with chopped parsley.
- Serve immediately.

In a pan over high heat, cook mussels until they open, which indicates that they are cooked.

Pour cream into strained broth, bring to the boil and allow to reduce slightly.

Whisk in butter cubes, one at a time, to finish the sauce.

Step-By-Step

MUSSELS WITH WHITE WINE
(MOULES MARINIERES)

Mussels are inexpensive and prepared in many ways throughout France. This traditional recipe is also the simplest way to prepare fresh mussels.

Ingredients

Mussels	2 kg (4 lb 6 oz)
Butter	50 g (2 oz)
Shallots	4, peeled and finely chopped
Garlic	2 cloves, peeled and finely chopped
Dry white wine	375 ml (12 fl oz / 1 1/2 cups)
Thyme	6 sprigs + extra for garnishing
Salt	to taste
Ground white pepper	to taste
Double (heavy) cream	300 ml (10 fl oz / 1 1/4 cups)
Cold butter	30 g (1 oz), cubed

Method

- Scrape mussels clean and remove beards. Once cleaned, rinse well under cold water and drain.
- Melt butter in a saucepan large enough for all the mussels. Add shallots and garlic and sauté until soft.
- Add wine, thyme and seasoning. Simmer for 3 minutes, then increase heat and add mussels.
- Cook mussels over high heat, shaking the saucepan often so that the mussels will open up.
- Remove opened mussels with a slotted spoon and discard those unopened.
- Strain cooked broth through a fine sieve and wipe down empty saucepan with paper towels.
- Return strained broth to saucepan and place over high heat for about 2 minutes.
- Whisk in cold butter, a piece at a time.
- Divide mussels among individual serving bowls and pour sauce over.
- Serve garnished with fresh thyme, if using.

Place bread slices into a bowl and add wine. Leave to soak until needed.

Fill squid tubes with prepared stuffing, then close opening and secure with 2 bamboo skewers or cocktail sticks, trimming off any excess.

Brown stuffed squid tubes in olive oil. Add tomato sauce and bake for 1–1½ hours.

Step-By-Step

STUFFED SQUID
(CHIPIRONS FARCIS)

The tangy taste of tomatoes make a perfect foil for the richly flavourful stuffing of shallots, garlic, ham and fresh herbs.

Ingredients

Squids	6, large, or 10–12 medium-size
Extra virgin olive oil	4 Tbsp
Red onion	1, peeled and finely chopped
Canned tomatoes	450 g (1 lb), chopped
Salt	to taste
Freshly ground black pepper	to taste
Bamboo skewers or cocktail sticks	

Stuffing

White sliced bread	70 g (2½ oz), crusts removed
White wine	85 ml (2½ fl oz / ⅓ cup)
Olive oil	90 ml (3 fl oz / 6 Tbsp)
Shallots	6, peeled and finely chopped
Garlic	2 cloves, peeled and finely chopped
Ham or prosciutto	280 g (10 oz), chopped
Chopped parsley	2 Tbsp + extra for garnishing
Chopped thyme	2 Tbsp + extra for garnishing
Egg	1, beaten, preferably free-range

Method

- Wash squids under cold running water. Cut off and reserve tentacles, then remove and discard heads, quills, wings and purple skins.
- Gently turn squid tubes inside out to clean, then turn back and pat dry with paper towels. Chop tentacles finely and set aside.
- Prepare tomato sauce. Heat olive oil in a saucepan and sauté onion until softened.
- Add canned tomatoes and seasoning. Reduce heat to low and cook for about 15 minutes, then remove from heat.
- Prepare stuffing. Put bread slices into a bowl and add wine. Leave to soak.
- Heat 2 Tbsp olive oil in a frying pan (skillet). Sauté shallots and garlic briefly, then add ham or prosciutto, tentacles, herbs and seasoning to taste. Cook for 5 minutes. Remove from heat.
- Add soaked bread slices to pan ingredients. Break them up and blend them into mixture with a fork. Leave to cool, then mix in beaten egg.
- Spoon stuffing into squid tubes. Secure openings with bamboo skewers or cocktail sticks.
- Heat remaining olive oil in a pan. Lightly brown squid tubes on all sides, then transfer to a baking dish or casserole.
- Add tomato sauce and bake in a preheated oven at 180°C (350°F) for 1–1½ hours, depending on size of squids. Turn them from time to time.
- If serving warm, leave squid tubes whole and serve garnished with herbs.
- If serving cold, slice squids into 2-cm (1-inch) rounds, place on serving plates and spoon sauce over to serve. Garnish as desired.

LANGOUSTINES IN CURRY SAUCE
(LANGOUSTINES AU CURRY)

The presence of curried sauces in a few French dishes is a legacy of the historical spice trade, which, for France, took place mainly in the Indies.

Ingredients

Langoustines or lobsters	1 kg (2 lb 3 oz)
Butter	70 g (2 1/2 oz)
Shallots	6, peeled and finely chopped
Garlic	2 cloves, peeled and finely chopped
Salt	to taste
Freshly ground black pepper	to taste
Thyme	6 sprigs, chopped
Parsley	6 sprigs, finely chopped
Curry powder	2 tsp
Calvados (apple brandy)	4 Tbsp
White wine	250 ml (8 fl oz / 1 cup)
Crème fraîche	250 ml (8 fl oz / 1 cup)
Asparagus	500 g (1 lb 1 1/2 oz) sliced into 0.5-cm (1/4-inch) pieces, blanched and refreshed

Step-By-Step

Shell blanched langoustines carefully to retain as much of their flavourful juices as possible.

Add calvados to pan and allow it to evaporate before adding wine and reserved juices. Calvados is a brandy made from apples and is a speciality of Normandy.

Whisk in crème fraîche and reduce sauce for 5 minutes before adding langoustines and asparagus.

Method

- Blanch langoustines in boiling water for 1 minute. Drain and leave to cool. Shell langoustines, reserving the juices.
- Heat butter in a saucepan. Add shallots, garlic, seasoning, herbs and curry powder. Cook over low heat until well mixed.
- Add calvados and allow it to evaporate, then pour in wine and reserved juices. Cook until liquid is reduced by half.
- Add crème fraîche and whisk to combine. Reduce sauce for a further 5 minutes.
- Add langoustines and asparagus to the sauce. Simmer over low heat until heated through.
- Serve on a platter.

Cut lobster tails in half with kitchen shears and ease tail meat out of shells. Cut cooked meat into bite-size pieces. Wash and dry shells for serving later.

To prepare sauce, work flour into melted butter, then whisk in reduced stock. Finish sauce by whisking in cream and egg yolk mixture.

Mix lobster meat with half the *béchamel* sauce, then spoon into tail shells.

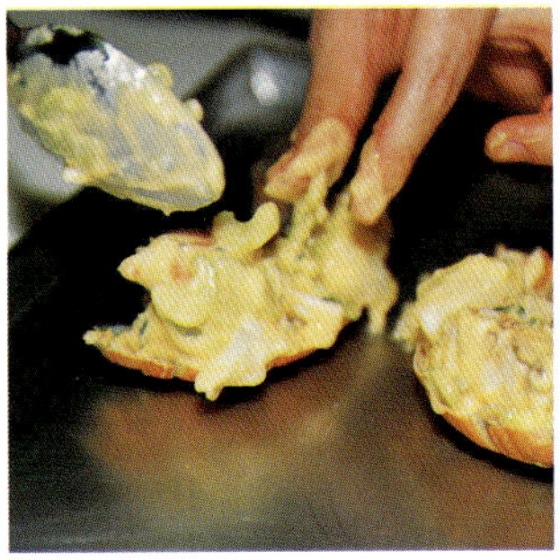

Step-By-Step

LOBSTER THERMIDOR

Napoleon named this dish after the month in which he first tasted it. Thermidor is the eleventh month of the French republican calendar.

Ingredients

Live lobsters	3, each about 500 g (1 lb 1½ oz)
Shallots	4, peeled and finely chopped
Garlic	2 cloves, peeled and finely chopped
Butter	125 g (4½ oz)
White wine	2 Tbsp
Fish stock	250 ml (8 fl oz / 1 cup)
Chopped tarragon	1 Tbsp
Plain (all-purpose) flour	2 Tbsp
Double (heavy) cream	250 ml (8 fl oz / 1 cup)
Egg yolks	2
Cayenne pepper	a pinch + extra for garnishing
Celery	½ rib, finely chopped
Finely grated Parmesan cheese	40 g (1¼ oz)

Method

- Lower lobsters, head first, into a stockpot of boiling water and boil for 3 minutes. Drain and leave to cool.
- Remove claws and knuckles of lobsters and reserve for another use.
- Twist off lobster tails, then halve each one lengthways. Ease meat out of the shells and cut into bite-size pieces. Wash shells and pat dry for serving later.
- Sauté shallots and garlic in 25 g (1 oz) butter until softened.
- Add wine, stock and tarragon. Reduce liquid over moderate heat by half. Remove from heat.
- Prepare *béchamel* sauce. Melt remaining butter in a saucepan and add flour. Stir until flour is completely incorporated.
- Add reduced stock, whisking until sauce is smooth and thickened.
- Combine cream and egg yolks in a small bowl.
- Remove sauce from heat and whisk in cream-and-yolk mixture with seasoning to taste and cayenne pepper.
- Mix chopped lobster meat with celery and half the *béchamel* sauce.
- Place lobster tails on a baking tray. Spoon lobster meat into the shells.
- Top with remaining sauce and cheese. Sprinkle cayenne pepper over to garnish.
- Place under a preheated oven-grill until golden brown.
- Serve immediately.

BOURRIDE OF SNAPPER, SÈTE-STYLE

Originating from the little fishing port of Sète, this recipe is customarily prepared with monk fish, but snapper is used here.

Ingredients

Olive oil	4 Tbsp
Butter	50 g (2 oz)
Salt	to taste
Freshly ground black pepper	to taste
Snapper fillets	6, each about 280 g (10 oz)
Carrots	2, peeled if desired and finely chopped
Celery leaves	12, finely chopped
Leeks	2, use only white parts, finely chopped
Spinach	200 g (7 oz), sliced

Sauce

Garlic	2 cloves, peeled and finely chopped
Dijon mustard	1 Tbsp
Egg yolks	2, extra-large, preferably free-range
Salt	a pinch
Olive oil	180 ml (6 fl oz / 3/4 cup)

Step-By-Step

Sear seasoned snapper fillets on both sides to seal in their juices, then remove and set aside until needed.

After sautéing vegetables, place seared fish fillets on top, cover pan and leave to cook for about 3 minutes or longer if fillets are thick.

Prepare sauce of garlic, mustard, egg yolks and salt. Whisk in olive oil, which is added in a thin stream.

Method

- Heat olive oil and butter in a frying pan (skillet) over moderate heat. Season fillets with salt and pepper and seal (sear) on both sides. Dish out and set aside.
- Add carrots, celery leaves and leeks. Season to taste and sauté for a few minutes, then add spinach and sauté until slightly softened.
- Return fish to pan, placing on top of vegetables. Cover, reduce heat slightly and leave to cook for 3 minutes, depending on the thickness of fillets.
- Meanwhile, prepare sauce. Combine garlic, mustard, egg yolks and salt in a large, shallow bowl.
- Add oil in a thin stream, whisking until mixture is firm.
- Transfer cooked fish to a platter and add sauce to vegetables in the pan, whisking to mix well. Add a splash of water if dry.
- Coat fish pieces with the sauce and serve immediately.

SEA BASS WITH STUFFING
(BAR FARCI)

Ingredients used to stuff whole fish vary slightly from region to region in France. Here, the herby flavours of fennel and chervil are prominent.

Ingredients

Sea bass	1.5 kg (3 lb 4 1/2 oz)
Butter	100 g (3 1/2 oz), cubed
Shallots	6, peeled and finely chopped
Button mushrooms	250 g (9 oz), finely chopped
Fennel bulb	1, finely chopped
Spinach	400 g (13 1/2 oz), finely chopped
Salt	to taste
Freshly ground black pepper	to taste
Breadcrumbs	55 g (2 oz)
Chervil	100 g (3 1/2 oz), finely chopped
Double (heavy) cream	200 ml (6 1/2 fl oz)
Dry vermouth	90 ml (3 fl oz / 6 Tbsp)

Step-By-Step

Ask the fishmonger to first scale and gut fish, then cut along the belly to open up butterfly-style and remove the backbone.

After seasoning the inside of fish, spoon stuffing ingredients on top, fold fish halves together and tie with kitchen string to secure, if necessary.

Place filled fish onto a baking tray and add cream mixture. Lastly, top with butter cubes before baking. Sprinkle with more salt to taste, if necessary.

Method

- Ask fishmonger to scale and gut fish, then open up fish along the belly without separating the two fillets and remove central bone. At home, rinse and pat dry fish.
- Prepare stuffing. Melt half the butter in a 25-cm (10-inch) non-stick pan and sauté shallots over low heat until soft.
- Add mushrooms, fennel, spinach and seasoning. Cook for 5 minutes, then mix in breadcrumbs and chervil.
- Season insides of fish with salt and pepper, then spoon stuffing onto one side. Fold over to cover, then transfer to a baking tray.
- Combine cream and vermouth and spoon mixture over fish. Dot fish with remaining butter.
- Bake in a preheated oven at 200°C (400°F) for about 30 minutes, depending on the size of the fish. Turn over halfway through cooking time.
- Serve immediately.

Place a salmon fillet on each paper circle, sprinkle with herbs and add a slice of lemon, then add seasoning to taste and 20 g (3/4 oz) butter on top.

To seal in fish and seasoning ingredients, fold paper circle in half again, then fold sections of semi-circular edge twice to secure.

Place paper parcels on a baking tray and bake in a preheated oven at 200°C/400°F for 10–12 minutes. When cooked, fish should be firm to the touch.

Step-By-Step

SALMON BAKED IN PAPER WITH BASIL SAUCE *(SAUMON AU PISTOU EN PAPILLOTE)*

The distinctive flavour of salmon combines well with the mixture of herbs and butter in this deeply aromatic dish.

Ingredients

Greaseproof paper	4 circles, each 30 cm (12 inches) in diameter
Butter	100 g (3 1/2 oz), cut into 5 equal pieces, each 20 g (3/4 oz)
Salmon fillets	4, each about 200 g (7 oz)
Finely chopped tarragon	2 Tbsp
Finely chopped chives	2 Tbsp
Finely chopped parsley	2 Tbsp
Finely chopped fennel	3 Tbsp
Lemon	1, thinly sliced
Salt	to taste
Ground white pepper	to taste
Garlic	1 clove, peeled and finely chopped
Basil leaves	20
Extra virgin olive oil	250 ml (8 fl oz / 1 cup)

Method

- Fold each greaseproof paper circle in half and smooth out again. Brush all 4 sheets with 20 g (3/4 oz) melted butter.
- Place a salmon fillet on one half of a paper circle. Sprinkle chopped herbs over fish and top with lemon slices. Season to taste.
- Place 20 g butter over each fillet, then fold paper over and seal.
- Place parcels on a baking tray and bake in a preheated oven at 200°C (400°F) for 10–12 minutes, depending on the thickness of the fillets.
- Prepare sauce. Combine garlic and basil in a blender (processor). Add seasoning to taste, then add oil gradually with blender still whirring.
- Serve each salmon parcel on a plate with basil sauce in a separate bowl.
- The aroma of salmon and herbs will delight diners as they open the parcels.
- Alternatively, transfer parcels to individual serving plates, then open up and spoon sauce over to serve.

Chicken Casserole (*Coq au Vin*)

Duck with Orange and Caramel Sauce

Rabbit with Mustard Sauce

Burgundy Beef (*Boeuf Bourguignon*)

Pepper Steak (*Steak au Poivre*)

Pork with Prunes (*Porc aux Prunes*)

Rack of Lamb Provençal

Veal Chops, Normandy Style (*Côtes de Veau Normandes*)

MEAT & POULTRY

Cut each cleaned chicken into 6–8 joints, then marinate with red wine, herbs and seasoning.

Drain marinated chicken and pat dry with paper towels, then coat lightly with plain flour, shaking off any excess, before sautéing until golden brown.

Beurre manié literally translates into "kneaded butter" and refers to a paste of blended softened butter and flour that acts as a thickener.

Step-By-Step

CHICKEN CASSEROLE
(COQ AU VIN)

A robust Burgundy red wine adds to the richness of this dish, which, according to legend, was created by the cook of Julius Caesar.

Ingredients

Chickens	2, each 1.5 kg (3 lb $4^1/_2$ oz), preferably free-range
Salt	to taste
Freshly ground black pepper	to taste
Olive oil	4 Tbsp
Butter	55 g (2 oz)
Pickling onions	20, peeled
Bacon	280 g (10 oz), chopped
Button mushrooms	280 g (10 oz), left whole
Plain (all-purpose) flour	$1^1/_2$ Tbsp + for dusting
Cognac	90 ml (3 fl oz / 6 Tbsp)
Tomato paste	1 Tbsp
Softened butter	2 Tbsp
Chopped parsley	4 Tbsp

Marinade

Red wine	750 ml (24 fl oz / 3 cups)
Thyme	6 sprigs
Rosemary	6 sprigs + extra for garnishing
Dried bay leaves	3

Method

- Cut each chicken into 6–8 joints and put into a large bowl. Add marinade ingredients and seasoning to taste. Refrigerate overnight.
- Heat oil and butter in a large casserole. Sauté onions, bacon and mushrooms for about 5 minutes, adding seasoning to taste. Dish out and set aside.
- Drain chicken pieces, reserving marinade, and pat dry with paper towels, then dust with flour.
- Sauté floured chicken in casserole until golden brown.
- Sprinkle in cognac and ignite, shaking casserole gently until the flames subside.
- Add marinade and tomato paste. Simmer over low heat for 35 minutes.
- Add mushroom mixture and cook for a further 30 minutes or until chicken is cooked through.
- Remove chicken and arrange on a serving platter. Remove and discard herbs from sauce.
- Mix together softened butter and $1^1/_2$ Tbsp flour to make a *beurre manié* and whisk into the sauce. Stir for 2 minutes or until sauce thickens.
- Add chopped parsley, then pour sauce over chicken.
- Garnish with extra rosemary, if desired and serve with garlic French bread.

Prick the skin of the cleaned and dried duck all over with a fork to release the fat from under the skin during cooking.

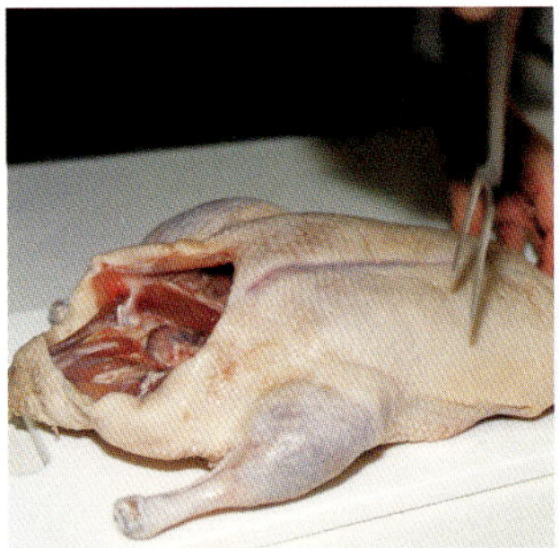

After roasting for 70 minutes, the duck's skin should be crisp and starting to brown. Brush duck with basting mix before roasting for another 30 minutes.

Remove cooked duck from oven and allow to rest a while before carving. It should be a rich brown colour, crisp outside and tender inside.

Step-By-Step

DUCK WITH ORANGE AND CARAMEL SAUCE

This dish may require considerable time and effort to prepare, but the reward is a richly tasty and utterly satisfying meal.

Ingredients

Duck	1, 2 kg (4 lb 6 oz), giblets removed, washed and dried
Salt	to taste
Freshly ground black pepper	to taste
Carrot	1, peeled and chopped
Onion	1, medium, peeled and halved
Parsley	2 sprigs
Dried thyme	2 tsp, or 1/2 sprig fresh
Garlic	2 cloves, left whole and unpeeled, lightly crushed
Cooking oil for greasing	
Rosemary (optional) for garnishing	

Basting Mix (combined)

Honey	2 Tbsp
Brown sugar	2 Tbsp
Ground cinnamon	1/2 tsp
Cointreau or other orange-flavoured liqueur	4 Tbsp

Method

- Prick cleaned duck all over with a fork, then season, inside and out, with salt and pepper.
- Stuff duck with carrot, onion, parsley, thyme and garlic.
- Oil the rack of the roasting pan and place duck on top, breast side up.
- Roast uncovered in a preheated oven at 170°C (340°F) for 40 minutes.
- Turn duck over and continue to roast for 30 minutes. The skin should be getting crisp and just beginning to brown.
- Remove duck from oven and generously brush with basting mix.
- Return duck to oven, increase heat to 190°C (370°F) and roast for a further 30 minutes, basting every now and then, until duck is a rich dark brown colour, and crisp and tender.
- Meanwhile, prepare orange sauce (see next page).
- When duck is cooked and orange sauce is ready, carve the duck.
- Arrange carved duck on a serving platter. Pour orange sauce over and serve.

Orange Sauce

Sugar	2 Tbsp
Red wine vinegar	4 Tbsp
Cooking oil	1 Tbsp
Duck bones	2 lower wings + neck
Beef stock	500 ml (16 fl oz / 2 cups)
Orange peel	from 2 oranges, julienned, simmered in boiling water for 15 minutes and drained
Port	180 ml (6 fl oz / $^{3}/_{4}$ cup)
Salt	to taste
Freshly ground black pepper	to taste
Corn flour (cornstarch)	1 Tbsp, mixed with 1 Tbsp water

Method

- Bring sugar and vinegar to the boil in a small, heavy saucepan. Reduce quickly to a mahogany brown syrup.
- Heat oil in another heavy saucepan over high heat and brown duck parts. Pour away excess fat.
- Stir in half the stock and heat through.
- Remove and discard duck parts, then add syrup and simmer for 1 minute.
- Add remaining stock, orange peel and port. Simmer for 20 minutes.
- Season to taste, thicken with corn flour paste and remove from heat.

RABBIT WITH MUSTARD SAUCE

Rabbit is very popular in France and is cooked in various ways. The combination of mustard and sage gives this dish its distinctive flavour.

Ingredients

Rabbit	1.5 kg (3 lb 4$^1/_2$ oz), cut into 8 pieces
Salt	to taste
Freshly ground black pepper	to taste
Cooking oil	85 ml (2$^1/_2$ fl oz / $^1/_3$ cup)
Butter	25 g (1 oz)
Strong French mustard	4 Tbsp
Button mushrooms	280 g (10 oz)
Sage	100 g (3$^1/_2$ oz), chopped
White wine	85 ml (2$^1/_2$ fl oz / $^1/_3$ cup)
Chicken stock	180 ml (6 fl oz / $^3/_4$ cup)
Crème fraîche	125 ml (4 fl oz / $^1/_2$ cup), or double (heavy) cream
Egg yolks	2

Step-By-Step

Cut rabbit into 8 pieces and season to taste with salt and pepper before browning in casserole.

After adding mustard, mushrooms, sage and wine to rabbit, reduce liquid by half before adding stock.

Remove cooked rabbit and mushrooms from casserole and make a sauce from pan juices by whisking in crème fraîche and egg yolks.

Method

- Season rabbit with salt and pepper.
- Heat oil and butter in a large casserole. Brown rabbit pieces on both sides.
- Add mustard, mushrooms and sage, then pour in wine and reduce by half.
- Slowly add stock, then cover and simmer over a low heat for 40 minutes.
- Remove cooked rabbit and mushrooms from casserole and keep warm.
- Mix together crème fraîche and egg yolks, then whisk into sauce left in casserole. Simmer gently for 5 minutes or until sauce thickens.
- Coat rabbit pieces with sauce and serve immediately.

BURGUNDY BEEF
(BOEUF BOURGUIGNON)

This beef stew recipe hails from Burgundy and is best made a day in advance for the rich flavours to develop.

Ingredients

Beef top round (topside) or chuck (shoulder)	1.8 kg (4 lb)
Cooking oil	4 Tbsp
Butter	50 g (2 oz)
Streaky bacon	125 g ($4\frac{1}{2}$ oz)
Pickling onions	20, small, peeled
Salt	to taste
Freshly ground black pepper	to taste
Plain (all-purpose) flour	3 Tbsp
Brandy	85 ml ($2\frac{1}{2}$ fl oz / $\frac{1}{3}$ cup)
Button mushrooms	280 g (10 oz)
Carrots	2, peeled if desired and chopped
Corn flour (cornstarch)	2 Tbsp, mixed with 2 Tbsp water

Marinade

Burgundy wine	750 ml (24 fl oz / 3 cups)
Garlic	3 cloves, peeled and finely chopped
Thyme	6 sprigs
Flat-leaf (Italian) parsley	8 sprigs

Step-By-Step

Combine beef and marinade ingredients in a large bowl, cover with cling film (plastic wrap) and refrigerate overnight.

Drain marinated beef in a colander set over pot. Discard herbs and garlic, but reserve marinade and set aside.

Pour brandy into casserole. When brandy has reduced for a few minutes, add reserved marinade and fried beef, then simmer for $1\frac{1}{2}$ hours.

Method

- Cut beef into 5-cm (2-inch) cubes. Combine beef and marinade ingredients in a large bowl and refrigerate overnight.
- Drain beef, reserving the marinade, and pat dry with paper towels. Set aside.
- Heat half the oil and butter in a large casserole. Brown bacon and remove with a slotted spoon. Set aside.
- Add remaining oil and butter, then onions and sauté over low heat until golden. Remove with a slotted spoon and add to bacon.
- Season beef to taste and lightly coat with flour, shaking off excess.
- Cook floured beef in batches until lightly browned, about 5 minutes. Turn meat frequently and add some butter or olive oil, if dry. Set aside.
- Pour out excess fat from casserole, then add brandy and reduce for a few minutes.
- Add marinade and meat. Simmer for about $1\frac{1}{2}$ hours, stirring occasionally.
- Add mushrooms, carrots, bacon and onions. Cook over low heat for 45 minutes or until beef is tender.
- Remove solid ingredients with a slotted spoon and set aside.
- Bring sauce left behind to the boil. Add corn flour paste and whisk through until sauce thickens.
- Reduce heat and return solid ingredients to casserole for 2 minutes to reheat and coat with sauce.
- Serve immediately.

PEPPER STEAK
(STEAK AU POIVRE)

Steak au poivre has become one of the classic dishes of French cuisine and is traditionally served with *pomme frittes*.

Ingredients

Beef tenderloin (fillet) steaks	4, each about 200 g (7 oz)
Olive oil	3 Tbsp
Salt	a pinch
Cracked black peppercorns	6 Tbsp
Butter	70 g ($2^1/_2$ oz)
Cognac	4 Tbsp
Crème fraîche	125 ml (4 fl oz / $^1/_2$ cup), or double (heavy) cream

Step-By-Step

Rub steaks on both sides with olive oil and season with salt before coating with cracked peppercorns.

Melt butter in a large frying pan (skillet) or grill pan until foamy, then cook seasoned steaks in it for 3 minutes on each side.

Remove steaks from pan, add crème fraîche and cook over high heat for 1 minute or until blended with pan juices.

Method

- Ask the butcher to cut the tenderloin or fillet into 200 g (7 oz) portions.
- Rub steaks on both sides with olive oil and season with salt, then rub in cracked peppercorns.
- Melt butter in a large frying pan (skillet) or grill pan. Cook steaks for 3–4 minutes on each side.
- Pour cognac over and ignite. When the flames subside, remove steaks from pan.
- Add crème fraîche and cook over high heat for 1 minute or until incorporated, stirring continuously.
- Serve steaks with sauce immediately.

Slice pork tenderloin into *noisettes*, or small rounds, for this dish. After slicing, stand each round on a cut side and press down to flatten.

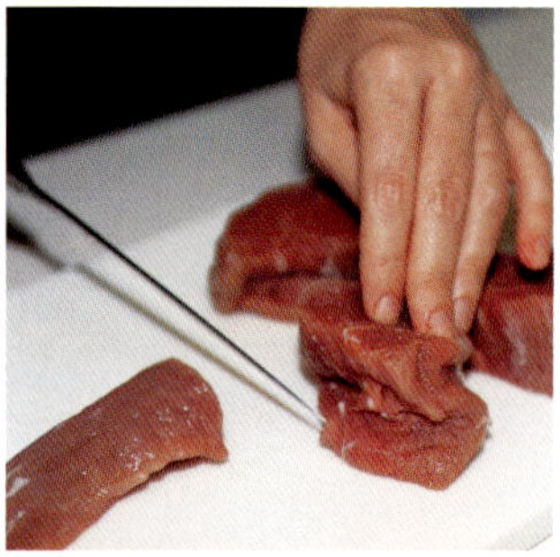

Slit each prune and remove stone inside if still attached, then boil pitted prunes in water to soften and drain.

Fill each prune with prepared stuffing, then set aside until needed.

Step-By-Step

PORK WITH PRUNES
(PORC AUX PRUNES)

Prunes and apples are often combined with pork. The sweetness of the fruits adds flavour and a certain lift to the dish.

Ingredients

Dried prunes	20, pitted
Butter	70 g (2 1/2 oz)
Walnuts	10, finely chopped
Shallots	4, peeled and finely chopped
Bacon	125 g (4 1/2 oz), finely chopped
Sage	55 g (2 oz), chopped finely
Salt	to taste
Freshly ground black pepper	to taste
Pork tenderloin (fillet)	1 kg (2 lb 3 oz), sliced into 200 g (7 oz) *noisettes*
Dry white wine	150 ml (5 fl oz)
Double (heavy) cream	250 ml (8 fl oz / 1 cup)

Method

- Make a single slit in each prune and remove stone if still attached.
- Put prunes into a small saucepan and add enough cold water to immerse. Bring to the boil and sustain for 2 minutes, then drain.
- Prepare stuffing. Melt half the butter and sauté walnuts, shallots, bacon and sage. Season to taste, then remove from heat.
- Fill each prune with stuffing. Set aside.
- Heat remaining butter in a clean frying pan (skillet) until foamy.
- Season pork to taste and brown both sides, then remove to a plate and keep warm.
- Pour out excess fat from pan, add wine and reduce.
- Add cream and simmer for a further 6 minutes or until sauce thickens.
- Add stuffed prunes, reserving a few for garnishing, and pork to sauce. Simmer until heated through.
- Serve with boiled parsley potatoes, if desired.

To save time, prepare crust mixture by pulsing ingredients in a blender (processor) until coarsely chopped, but not puréed.

Seal and brown lamb in melted butter, then remove and cool to room temperature.

Spread a little mustard onto each piece of lamb before coating with crust mixture.

Step-By-Step

RACK OF LAMB PROVENÇAL

Flavourful lamb served with a selection of spring vegetables, including asparagus, new potatoes and squash, makes a heartwarming meal.

Ingredients

Racks of lamb	3, each about 300 g (10 oz)
Butter	50 g (2 oz)
Dijon mustard	1 Tbsp
Olive oil	1 Tbsp

Crust Mixture (combined)

Garlic	4 cloves, peeled and finely chopped
Lemon zest	grated from 1 lemon
Salt	2 tsp
Dijon mustard	1 tsp
Soft green peppercorns	1 tsp, chopped
Rosemary	8 sprigs, finely chopped
Oregano	8 sprigs, finely chopped
Marjoram	8 sprigs, finely chopped

Method

- Preheat oven to 220°C (440°F).
- Wipe and pat dry meat with paper towels.
- Heat butter in a frying pan (skillet). When it starts to foam, add lamb and seal all sides.
- When lamb is golden brown, remove and leave to cool to room temperature.
- Spread a little mustard onto each piece of lamb, then coat generously with crust mixture and drizzle with olive oil.
- Place racks of lamb on a roasting pan and roast in the oven at 200°C (400°F) for 15–20 minutes.
- Remove lamb from oven and allow to rest for 5 minutes.
- Carve meat into slices and serve with spring vegetables.

VEAL CHOPS, NORMANDY STYLE
(CÔTES DE VEAU NORMANDES)

This dish of tender veal and sweet apples is well-complemented and made substantial with the accompaniment of creamed potatoes.

Ingredients

Golden delicious (yellow) apples	3, peeled and cored
Butter	85 g (3 oz)
Veal chops	4–6, each about 200 g (7 oz)
Salt	to taste
Freshly ground black pepper	to taste
Calvados (apple brandy)	4 Tbsp
Crème fraîche	250 ml (8 fl oz / 1 cup), or double (heavy) cream

Step-By-Step

Peel, core and halve apples, then cut each piece into 3 equal slices.

Cook apple pieces in half the butter over moderate heat until golden, then dish out and set aside.

To serve, remove cooked veal chops to a platter and add apples, then pour sauce over.

Method

- Peel and core apples, then halve each one. Slice each half into 3 equal wedges.
- Melt half the butter in a non-stick pan and cook apples over moderate heat until golden. Remove from pan.
- Add remaining butter to pan. Season veal and sauté over moderate heat for 5 minutes on each side.
- Remove veal from pan, then add calvados and cook until evaporated.
- Add crème fraîche and reduce by half, whisking constantly until sauce is of coating consistency. Remove from heat.
- Arrange veal chops on a serving platter and place apples around, then spoon sauce over.
- Serve dish with creamed potatoes, if desired.

Chocolate Mousse (*Mousse au Chocolat*)

Pears in Red Wine (*Poires au Vin*)

Apple Tart (*Tarte aux Pommes*)

Vanilla Custard with Caramel Sauce

Date and Walnut Meringue Cream Cookies

Flourless Chocolate Cake (*Le Nègre*)

DESSERTS

CHOCOLATE MOUSSE
(MOUSSE AU CHOCOLAT)

Chocolate mousse is a decadently rich dessert and a fitting way to end off a memorable meal.

Ingredients

Dark chocolate	300 g (10$^1/_2$ oz), broken into pieces, use best quality available
Eggs	5, separated
Double (heavy) cream	500 ml (16 fl oz / 2 cups)
Castor (superfine) sugar	2 Tbsp
Grand marnier or cognac	2 Tbsp

Step-By-Step

Break chocolate into small pieces and place into a bain-marie, then melt over gentle heat until fluid.

Add a large, heaped spoonful of beaten egg whites and fold into chocolate mixture.

Spoon mousse into desired serving cups and refrigerate for 2–3 hours or until set.

Method

- Melt chocolate in bain-marie or double-boiler over gentle heat until fluid.
- Remove from heat and leave to cool to room temperature.
- Meanwhile, beat egg whites until stiff and set aside.
- Whisk cream to soft peak stage. Add sugar and whisk further until sugar is incorporated. Set aside.
- Lightly beat egg yolks and stir into chocolate, then add liqueur or cognac and mix until smooth.
- Fold a heaped spoonful of beaten egg whites into chocolate mixture; this helps to lighten it.
- Fold lightened chocolate into remaining egg whites.
- Finally, fold in sweetened cream.
- Spoon mousse into desired serving cups and refrigerate for 2–3 hours or until set.
- Before serving, remove from refrigerator and bring to room temperature for the texture to be soft and creamy.

PEARS IN RED WINE
(POIRES AU VIN)

This pretty dessert is rich, deep red in colour and can be served as an accompaniment to other desserts.

Ingredients

Chinese pears	12 small, or 5 large
Red wine	750 ml (24 fl oz / 3 cups)
Port	250 ml (8 fl oz / 1 cup)
Sugar	180 g (6 oz)
Orange zest	grated from 1 orange, washed and dried
Cinnamon stick	1, 9-cm (3½-inches) long
Vanilla bean	1, halved and seeds scraped out, or 1 tsp vanilla bean paste
Black peppercorns	4
Clove	1

Step-By-Step

Prepare wine syrup by combining all ingredients, except pears, in a saucepan and simmer for 5 minutes or until sugar is dissolved.

When wine syrup is ready, lower pears into it and cook, covered, for 20 minutes. Turn pears for even colouring, if necessary.

Ladle cooled syrup over only just before serving. This dessert goes well with fresh cream or vanilla ice-cream.

Method

- Peel pears carefully, leaving stems intact.
- Combine all ingredients, except pears, in a saucepan large enough to hold all the pears. Alternatively, cook in batches.
- Bring to the boil and simmer for 5 minutes.
- Add pears, cover and simmer gently for 20 minutes. Turn them to coat evenly with wine mixture, if necessary.
- Remove pears and leave to cool. Reduce sauce for 10 minutes to thicken slightly, then remove from heat and cool.
- Arrange pears on a shallow serving dish and pour sauce over just before serving.
- Serve with fresh cream or home-made vanilla ice-cream.

APPLE TART
(TARTE AUX POMMES)

As orchards overflow with fruit in late summer and autumn, many cooks take advantage of the harvest and use fruit in their desserts.

Ingredients

Egg yolks	4
Sugar	90 g (3 oz)
Vanilla bean paste	1/2 tsp, or 3 drops vanilla essence (extract)
Ground cinnamon	1/2 tsp
Double (heavy) cream	180 ml (6 fl oz / 3/4 cup)
Golden delicious (yellow) or pippin (green) apples	450 g (1 lb)
Icing (confectioner's) sugar (optional) for dusting	

Sweet Shortcrust Pastry

Soft butter	125 g (4 1/2 oz)
Castor (superfine) sugar	90 g (3 oz)
Egg	1
Plain (all-purpose) flour	250 g (9 oz)
Salt	a generous pinch

Step-By-Step

Knead dough until smooth and elastic, then wrap in plastic and refrigerate. To save time, buy frozen shortcrust pastry. Use 450 g (1 lb) for this recipe.

Arrange apple slices in a circular fashion on top of pastry in the tart tin.

While tart is in the oven for the first 15 minutes, beat egg yolks, sugar, vanilla bean paste and cinnamon together in a cake mixer, then beat in cream until stiff peaks form.

Method

- Prepare pastry. Cream butter and sugar until pale and fluffy.
- Add egg and mix for 30 seconds, then add flour and salt. Mix until a smooth dough forms.
- Place dough on a clean work surface and knead—push it out with the palm of your hand, then reform into a ball. Knead until dough is smooth and elastic.
- Wrap dough in plastic and chill for at least 2 hours or preferably longer. Remove from refrigerator 1 hour before using.
- Butter a fluted 25-cm (10-inch) tart tin. Roll out pastry into a 30-cm (12-inch) circle and line tart tin.
- Bake pastry blind (see pg 41) for 10 minutes on the bottom shelf, then remove and leave to cool completely.
- Meanwhile, beat egg yolks, sugar, vanilla paste and cinnamon in a bowl until mixture is pale. Alternatively, use a cake mixer for 3–4 minutes.
- Add cream and continue beating until stiff peaks form. Set aside.
- Peel, core and quarter apples. Cut each quarter into 3–4 slices lengthways, depending on size of apples.
- Dry apple slices then arrange evenly and in a circular fashion on top of pastry.
- Pour cream mixture over apple slices and bake in a preheated oven at 170°C (340°F) for 30–35 minutes or until apples slices are tender.
- Remove tart from oven and cool. Dust surface with icing sugar, if using, before serving.

Bring milk and vanilla to the boil over low heat, stirring constantly with a balloon whisk. Once boiled, remove from heat and leave to cool.

Grease 6 ramekins, each about 6-cm ($2\frac{1}{2}$-inch) deep and 6-cm ($2\frac{1}{2}$-inch) in diameter, with some cooking oil before adding caramel.

Strain custard mixture through a fine sieve and skim off any froth before filling moulds or ramekins.

Step-By-Step

VANILLA CUSTARD WITH CARAMEL SAUCE

A classic French dessert, *crème caramel* is a creamy, oven-baked custard with a light caramel sauce.

Ingredients

Full cream milk	600 ml (20 fl oz)
Vanilla bean paste	1 tsp or more to taste
Eggs	4, extra-large
Egg yolks	2, extra-large
Castor (superfine) sugar	125 ml (4 fl oz / $\frac{1}{2}$ cup)
Cooking oil for greasing moulds	

Syrup

Sugar	180 ml (6 fl oz / $\frac{3}{4}$ cup)
Water	85 ml ($2\frac{1}{2}$ fl oz / $\frac{1}{3}$ cup)
Fresh lemon juice	3 Tbsp

Method

- Prepare custard. Bring milk and vanilla to the boil in a heavy saucepan over low heat, stirring constantly.
- Remove from heat and set aside for about 45 minutes for flavours to infuse.
- Prepare syrup. Combine all ingredients in a small, heavy saucepan.
- Stir over moderate heat until sugar is dissolved, then allow to simmer, without stirring, until medium gold in colour.
- Meanwhile, grease 6 ovenproof ramekins. When caramel has reached the right colour, divide it equally among ramekins.
- Swirl each one so that caramel coats the entire base and some of the sides. Set aside.
- Whisk eggs, egg yolks and sugar in a mixing bowl or cake mixer until well combined.
- Add vanilla-infused milk, whisking continuously, then pass through a fine sieve. Skim off froth and divide equally among ramekins.
- Place filled ramekins in a baking pan and add hot water until they are half submerged.
- Loosely cover with aluminium foil and bake in a preheated oven at 160°C (325°F) for about 25 minutes.
- Turn custard and check water level, adding more if necessary.
- Bake for 20 minutes more or until custard is slightly wobbly at the centre.
- Remove from oven and remove foil, then leave to cool in the pan.
- Refrigerate overnight before serving. To serve, run a paring knife along the sides of each ramekin and turn out onto serving plates.

To prepare meringue, first beat egg whites until firm peaks form, then gradually beat in sugar until meringue is stiff; it should not move when bowl is tilted.

Using a large metal spoon, fold crumbed biscuits, dates and walnuts, into meringue. Ensure that ingredients are evenly distributed.

Using 2 tablespoons, fill marked circles with just enough meringue mixture to form chunky cookies.

Step-By-Step

DATE AND WALNUT MERINGUE CREAM COOKIES

This is a light dessert that goes well with good, strong coffee. Boudoir biscuits are also known as sponge biscuits or sponge fingers.

Ingredients

Egg whites	5, extra-large
Castor (superfine) sugar	125 g ($4^{1}/_{2}$ oz)
Boudoir biscuits	125 g ($4^{1}/_{2}$ oz), crushed into crumbs
Dried pitted dates	250 g (9 oz), coarsely chopped
Walnuts	250 ml (8 fl oz / 1 cup), coarsely chopped
Aluminium foil	
Butter for greasing	

Method

- Beat egg whites in a large mixing bowl or a cake mixer until firm peaks form.
- Add sugar gradually, beating until meringue is stiff and glossy.
- Use a large metal spoon to fold in crumbed biscuits, followed by dates, then walnuts.
- Line 2 baking trays with aluminium foil and lightly grease with butter.
- Take a cup with a 5-cm (2-inch) diameter and invert it to mark as many circles as each surface can accommodate.
- Spoon on sufficient meringue to cover each marked circle.
- Bake in a preheated oven at 180°C (350°F) for 10 minutes or until biscuits turn medium gold in colour.
- Remove from oven and leave to cool on the baking tray.
- When cool, they should be firm outside and soft and chewy inside.
- Store in an airtight container and refrigerate until needed.

Step-By-Step

Add half the sugar to egg yolks and whisk until it is pale in colour with a balloon whisk. Alternatively, combine using a cake mixer.

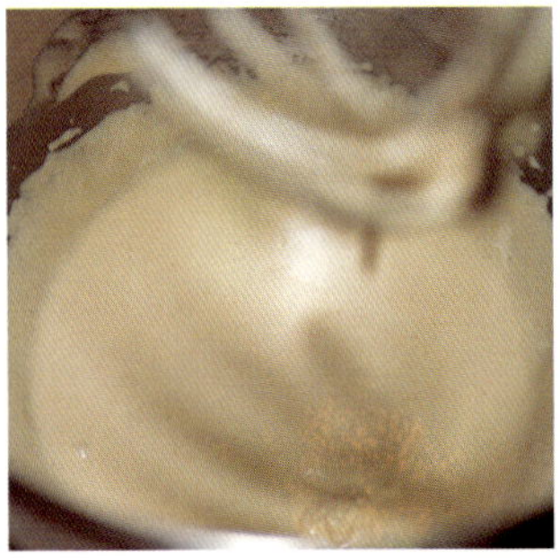

Beat egg whites until soft peaks form. Again, this can be done by hand with a mixing bowl and a balloon whisk or using a cake mixer.

To test if cake is ready, insert a skewer into the centre and if it comes out clean, the cake is ready.

FLOURLESS CHOCOLATE CAKE
(LE NÈGRE)

In not using flour, this recipe makes a very soft-textured cake. Serve warm with freshly whipped cream.

Ingredients

Dark chocolate	200 g (7 oz), preferably orange-infused
Soft butter	200 g (7 oz)
Sugar	200 g (7 oz) or more to taste
Eggs	4, large, preferably free-range, separated
Icing (confectioner's) sugar (optional) for dusting	

Method

- Break chocolate into small pieces and melt in a bain-marie or double-boiler. Remove from heat.
- Add butter and stir with a spatula until smooth. Set aside.
- Add half the sugar to egg yolks and whisk until mixture is pale in colour, then beat in chocolate mixture.
- Separately beat egg whites until soft peaks form. Gradually add remaining sugar, beating until smooth and shiny.
- Fold 2 rounded (heaped) Tbsp chocolate mixture into beaten egg whites.
- Gently fold egg white mixture into chocolate mixture with a slotted spoon.
- Pour batter into a greased, 22-cm (9-in) round cake pan.
- Bake on the centre shelf in a preheated oven at 190°C (370°F) for 40 minutes or until done.
- Dust surface with icing sugar, if using and slice to serve.

GLOSSARY OF INGREDIENTS

Basil
Intensely fragrant and part of the mint family, basil is widely used in Provençal cooking. It has a clove-like scent that is mostly lost when dried. The flavour of fresh basil can be preserved in a herb butter, oil or vinegar. Dried basil is, nevertheless, sometimes handy for use out of season.

Also known as sweet basil, the herb is a key ingredient in pistou, the Niçoise version of a Genoese pesto sauce. Pistou contains, in addition to basil, garlic, olive oil and Parmesan and is frequently added to pasta or soups and stews. Fresh basil leaves are an excellent way to liven up salads and have a well-known affinity with tomatoes. Basil also goes well with chicken, lamb and some oily fish. French cooks tend to use basil with leaves that are medium in size. The Italian variety of basil is large-leafed, while the Greek variety is small-leafed. Both, however, are useful in cooking. The purple-leafed opal basil, while less flavourful, makes a great decorative item in salads.

Bay Leaf
Part of the laurel family, the bay leaf (*Laurus nobilis*) has been described as a characteristic flavouring in French cooking. The fragrance of the leaf is slightly balsamic, with fresh bay leaves having been described as a delicate balance of lemon and nutmeg. When dried, bay leaves are spicier and more pungent; the flavour of a dried leaf is about twice as strong as a fresh one.

The bay leaf is used in all regions of France to flavour soups, stews, sauces and pâtés, as well as some sweet custards and creams. The herb is also one of the three that make up the classic bouquet garni, which also includes parsley and thyme.

Capers
Capers are the pickled flower buds of a small, tropical bush (*Capparis spinosa*) native to the Mediterranean region. They are piquant and pungent, and are often used as a seasoning for sauces, relishes and a variety of dishes involving fish, meat or vegetables.

Sold in jars all over France, capers are also sold loose in some of the country's markets, where they soak in wooden vats of brine. Many French sauces—gribiche, ravigote, tapénade, rémoulade and tartare—include capers.

If the buds are allowed to mature and bloom, they become white or pale-lilac flowers. The plant from which capers grow is part of the mustard family. Capers are cultivated in the Bouches-du-Rhone and the Var regions of France and tend to be smaller than those imported from Spain or North Africa.

Chervil
A member of the parsley family, chervil is widely used in French cooking. Used both as a seasoning and a garnish, the feathery leaves have a delicate flavour, which some have described as resembling parsley and aniseed. Chervil is typically added to soups or cooked vegetables and its tender leaves are delicious in salads. Chervil also makes excellent herb vinegar and is a component of fines herbes, a mixture of finely chopped herbs typically used to flavour an omelette or garnish grilled steak. If using dried chervil, crush it in the palm of your hand to release its flavour before adding to the dish.

Chickpeas
Also known as garbanzo beans, chickpeas are part of the pea family and they are creamy yellow in colour, with a mild, nutty flavour. Although most often sold dried, canned chickpeas are also available. These are ready-cooked and usually salted. Chickpeas keep their shape even with prolonged cooking, although they become less resistant to the bite and gain a more powdery texture. Dried chickpeas need to be soaked in water for several hours or preferably overnight to rehydrate them before cooking. Canned chickpeas, on the other hand, are already soft which reduces cooking time, but they have also lost a great deal of flavour.

Coriander
The presence of coriander in France and French cuisine is arguably a legacy of North African influence. A member of the parsley family, the coriander plant is sought after mainly for its fragrant leaves and flavourful fruit. Thai cooks are also known to use the roots. Coriander leaves, known as cilantro or Chinese parsley, are often used both as flavouring and as garnish. The herb is deeply and distinctively aromatic, and widely known as "coriander seeds", dried coriander fruit make a robust spice. Sold whole or ground, coriander 'seeds' are typically used to flavour pickles, cured meats or strong-tasting dishes. In fact, they are the key component in curry powders.

Chives
Chives come in long, thin shoots and have a delicate onion-flavour. Chives have been widely used in sauces and salads for centuries. Chives are, in fact, related to the onion and are part of the lily family. In terms of taste, chives have a certain affinity with eggs and cream. When finely chopped, they also make an attractive, bright green garnish. In the summer months, chive plants bloom with mauve flowers that are also edible. These flowers are frequently used to garnish salads.

Dill

Although dill is native to the Mediterranean region, it was rarely utilised in traditional French cooking. In fact, the original Larousse Gastronomique, a trusted and respected encyclopaedia on French cookery published in the nineteenth century, had no entry for it. In more recent times, cooks and chefs have experimented with the herb and brought about pleasing results—from the curing of raw fish, in particular salmon, *gravid lax* style to the flavouring of a vinaigrette for potatoes or a green salad. The fine feathery leaves of dill are distinctively aromatic and considered pungent to some. They generally do well in pickles, salads, sauces and soups.

Fennel

The seeds, stalks and feathery leaves of this anise-flavoured herb are used in cooking. Fennel is related to dill and is a member of the buttercup family. It comes in two main varieties, one green-leafed and the other bronze-leafed. Seeds of the herb are dried and also used in cooking. Fennel grows wild throughout Provence and is typically used in a bouquet garni for a court bouillon, which is a herbal stock used for poaching fish. Chopped fennel is often added to a sauce or mayonnaise. Sweet fennel is another variety and has a bulbous base. It is typically thinly sliced and eaten like celery.

Garlic

Garlic is used throughout France but especially so in the south, where it is grown. A member of the lily family, garlic comes in pods or "heads" that break down into wedge-like cloves. Garlic has a distinctively strong odour and taste. When sautéed in oil, it becomes deeply aromatic. In mid-summer, the freshly harvested green garlic, which has a less pungent flavour, is used to make soups. Garlic is used in a great many meat and fish dishes. It is also essential to aioli, the garlic-rich mayonnaise, and makes a fine-flavoured vinegar. Even on its own, simply peeled and slow roasted, garlic is tremendously flavourful.

Green Split Peas

Already split and without their skins, these peas are both nutritious and fast-to-cook. Typically used to make soups, these peas are known to the Indians as green *matar* dhal. Yellow split peas can be used if green ones are unavailable. Yellow peas have a stronger, earthier flavour, do not require soaking and cook quite quickly.

Haricot Beans
Creamy white in colour, these beans are typically used to make baked beans or added to soups. They require prolonged cooking to soften and break down, and are also quite hard to digest. The fact that they make diners feel full for a longer time may be one reason why these beans have been adopted by meal planners in the U.S. navy since the mid-1800s. For this reason, they are often also known as navy or white beans.

Juniper Berries
Juniper berries begin with a pale green colour on the tree and turn blue as they mature. They are a blackish blue when ripe and ready for picking. Usually found in the spice section of supermarkets, these small, black berries are sold dried and are deeply aromatic. Typically used to season poultry or game, whether as part of the marinade or stuffing, juniper berries also make a great flavouring agent for pickles and particularly robust pâtés or terrines. Crush the berries to release their flavour before using. The French know them as *baies de geniévre.*

Mint
The mint family of plants is large and different varieties grow throughout the world. However, the Mediterranean region is where mint clearly dominates the local vegetation like nowhere else. The flavour of mint is fresh, distinctive and pungent, making it a wonderful foil for lamb. Similarly, add a handful of tender mint leaves to a mixed green salad for lift and zest. After a heavy meal, serve some mint tea instead of coffee to aid digestion. The two most important commercial varieties of mint, and also the most well known, are peppermint and spearmint. The latter's flavour is said to be milder than the former but both are valued for the menthol they contain. Menthol is the oil that is drawn out from mint and goes a long way in flavouring medicine, chewing gum, candy and many other household products. In their natural states, spearmint can be differentiated from peppermint by its lack of a leafstalk.

Oregano

The name "oregano" is Greek for "joy of the mountain". Also known as wild marjoram, oregano is related to both marjoram and thyme and is part of the larger mint family. Oregano smells and tastes stronger than marjoram but is less sweet. Fresh or dried, oregano leaves make a great seasoning for tomatoes, cooked cheese dishes, robustly flavoured meats and pizzas. A Mexican variety of oregano exists. It is more pungent than its Mediterranean counterpart and is usually found dried in Latin markets.

Parsley

This is an important herb in French cookery, and probably the most often used. Parsley is a part of the classic bouquet garni and also fines herbes, which is a blend of finely chopped parsley, chives, tarragon and thyme that is used as a seasoning. Both the curly form (*frisé*) and the flat-leaf (*commun or d'Italie*) varieties are used in many dishes, whether as a seasoning or a garnish. Flat-leaf parsley is sometimes known as Italian parsley. Part of the carrot family, parsley is especially rich in vitamin C.

As is the case with most herbs, avoid chopping up parsley long in advance. This is because its flavour and aroma are considerably reduced if allowed to sit after cutting. Chopping up the herb just before adding it to the dish ensures that the full flavour of its aromatic oils are captured upon release. A cream sauce flavoured with only parsley has a freshness no other herb can match. Another case in point would be the persillade, which is a mixture of finely chopped parsley and shallots, as well as grated lemon zest that is added to a dish in the final stages of preparation.

Puy Lentils

Puy lentils are favoured by cooks around the world because of their robust flavour and their ability to keep their shape despite cooking. Native to France, they were originally grown in the country's region of Puy, where volcanic soils allowed the pulse to thrive. This explains why Puy lentils are sometimes known as French lentils, although they are also grown in North America and Italy today. Puy lentils require a longer cooking time compared to other types of lentils.

Rocket (Arugula) Leaves

Known to the French as *roquette* and Americans as arugula, rocket leaves are deep green in colour and curly. They have a distinctive, pungent taste that some have described as being rather like peanuts and others as peppery. They are typically added to mixed green salads, and just a few leaves would improve the flavour of most salads. Rocket leaves are included in the Provençal mixture of tender salad leaves known as mesclun, while its white flowers can be used to decorate a salad. Cultivation of rocket leaves began as recently as the 1990s. Previously, they were picked from the wild.

Rosemary

The plant from which rosemary leaves are derived is a member of the mint family and native to the Mediterranean region. It is also evergreen and quite hardy. Rosemary leaves are short and needle-shaped, grey-green in colour on the surface and whitish on the underside. Although small in size, rosemary leaves pack a punch in aroma and flavour, so much so that cooks should always use them sparingly. Fresh or dried, they could easily overpower a dish. Their pungency also means that they are often paired with similarly strong-tasting ingredients such as lamb, veal and poultry. Often, young branches of the herb are used as skewers for barbecued or oven-grilled foods, which include meat, fish and vegetables. Prepared this way, the skewered foods get just a hint of the distinctive rosemary aroma. Rosemary is one component of the herbes de Provence, which also includes basil, fennel seeds, lavender, marjoram, sage and thyme. The blend of herbs is regarded as characteristic of the flavours of southern France, where rosemary grows wild.

Sage

The sage leaves cooks add to their dishes come from an evergreen shrub that is native to southern Europe. Sage leaves are greyish-green in appearance and slightly bitter to the taste. They give off a distinctively strong aroma when cooked. Sold fresh and dried, sage is most commonly used to flavour sausages, as well as dishes involving poultry and meat such as pork, veal and lamb. Some cooks use the deep blue flowers from the sage plant to garnish salads. Although the herb is sold in both fresh and dried forms, fresh sprigs, if available, give the best effects with cooking. Dried sage leaves can develop a musty flavour over time and should be stored in a cool, dry place for no more than one year. Crush dried sage to release its flavour before using.

Thyme

A member of the mint family, thyme is a pleasantly pungent herb, with lots of tiny leaves. Several varieties of thyme, including common, wild and lemon, are used for cooking. The herb is used in a wide variety of usually meat-based dishes but always sparingly or at least with caution. This is because its flavour, while appetising, is also very strong and can overpower a dish if the cook has been heavy-handed. Thyme is sold fresh, dried and ground. It is also a part of the classic bouquet garni. France and Spain are the world's leading producers of thyme.

INDEX